THE THINGS

THAT ARE CAESAR'S

THE THINGS THAT ARE CAESAR'S

BY MILTON KATZ

NEW YORK · ALFRED A. KNOPF

1966

The epigraph to Chapter i is reprinted from *The History of Rome* by Theodor Mommsen with the permission of Meridian Books, The World Publishing Company.

The epigraph to Chapter iv, from "The Congo" by Vachel Lindsay, is reprinted with the permission of The Macmillan Company from his *Collected Poems*. Copyright 1914 The Macmillan Company; renewed 1942 by Elizabeth C. Lindsay.

The first epigraph to Chapter v is reprinted from *The British Civil Service* by Herman Finer with the permission of George Allen and Unwin Ltd.

The second epigraph to Chapter v is reprinted from *Eminent Victorians* by Lytton Strachey with the permission of Harcourt, Brace & World, Inc.

The epigraph to Chapter vi is reprinted from *A History of the English People, 1815–1915* by Elie Halévy with the permission of Harcourt, Brace & World, Inc.

The second epigraph to Chapter vii is reprinted from "A Shropshire Lad"—Authorized Edition—from *The Collected Poems of A. E. Housman*, Copyright 1939, 1940, © 1959 by Holt, Rinehart and Winston, Inc., with the permission of Holt, Rinehart and Winston, Inc., and of The Society of Authors as the literary representative of the Estate of the late A. E. Housman, and Messrs. Jonathan Cape Ltd.

FOR

ARTHUR M. SCHLESINGER

(*1888–1965*)

IN MEMORIAM

ACKNOWLEDGMENTS

I am indebted to the late Arthur M. Schlesinger, who encouraged my venture into this book and applied his wisdom to appraising it in an early draft. Thomas J. Wilson gave me the benefit of his advice from the beginning, and he and Crane Brinton were generous enough to read and criticize the manuscript. My son, Robert Katz, carried the main burden of preparing the index.

I want to thank the Carnegie Corporation of New York for a grant that provided precious time and secretarial and research assistance, and the Rockefeller Foundation for affording me the seclusion of the Villa Serbelloni at Bellagio, Italy, where I completed the final revision of the book.

CONTENTS

THE THINGS

THAT ARE CAESAR'S

TO WIN POWER AND TO GOVERN

. . . scarcely once in a thousand years does a man arise who is a king not merely in name but in fact.

Mommsen, *The History of Rome*

It takes qualities of one kind to face an electorate and win elective office in the United States today. It takes qualities of another kind to govern. Some men, a few, are abundantly endowed with both. Of these, some, even fewer, through time, chance, or personal inclination, put their gifts to work in politics and government. They are the nation's good fortune. Without them, America could not realize its potentialities nor achieve its purposes, but they are too few for government in America to fulfill its mission through them alone.

There are more who are amply equipped with qualities of the one kind or the other, but not both. Of these, some have the understanding and skill to perform the tasks required of government but are disinclined to run for office or unable to do so effectively. They will not "get into politics"; if and when they do, they "can't get elected." They can do the job, but they cannot get the job. Others ride the waves and currents of electoral politics with zest and dexterity. They readily establish communion with an

3

electorate and move triumphantly into office, but there the triumph begins and ends. The requirements of the office as an instrument of government are largely beyond them because of unawareness, indifference, or lack of appropriate talent or training. They can get the job, but they cannot do the job.

These are matters of degree, of course. To avoid misunderstanding, at this point let me risk laboring the obvious. If "no man is an island, entire of itself," so also no man—or hardly any—is neatly made of uniform paste. He is a composite, and we are concerned with the typical mix and the comparative measure of elements in the mix. Few politicians—if any—who can get the job are totally devoid of capacity or desire to do it. Few men —if any—who could do the job are wholly unable or unwilling to understand political power or do what must be done to win it. Even aside from the few to whom Nature has given talents and interests with both hands, there are many gifted and inclined in the one direction who have also some ability or propensity in the other. Some, but not enough. Along the one line or the other, their capacity or inclination typically falls short to a serious degree. They cannot meet both the needs of electoral politics and the needs of effective government in respect of the offices they seek or hold, or they are insufficiently concerned to try.

By a natural contagion, the disparities between the attributes that make for political success and those needed for effective government tend to spread from the elective sector to the appointive, for the power of appoint-

4

ment rests immediately or ultimately with the holders of political power. When those who get the job do not understand its needs and potentialities or do not care, their lack of knowledge or concern will tend to be reflected in the character of the personnel they appoint. When the winner of political power also has the capacity and will to govern, the prospect for the appointment of qualified personnel is much better. It is also measurably better when an elected officer, lacking the relevant skills or training to do the job, nevertheless appreciates the needs and possibilities. But even in such cases, forces inherent in the process by which the coveted place is won may frustrate or narrow the prospect. A man who wins elective office does not do so abruptly out of the blue, nor does he do it alone. The victory ordinarily culminates a period of effort in which he works with associates and helpers. Since the value of the supporting cast is gauged by their contribution to the electoral struggle, they are chosen for their appetite and flair for winning political power. Their other traits are incidental. They do not lose their appetite when their principal wins office, but file lusty claims for the subordinate posts within his appointive reach. By the standards of those occupied with political power, their claims have a kind of merit; and since their principal wants to keep, renew or extend his place, the merits are reinforced by his anticipation of a continuing need for their assistance. To the extent that their claims are satisfied, the room for appointments based upon capacity to govern is correspondingly reduced. The principal wins power and retains it with men of one kind; to govern, he needs another kind. It is hard to find room for both and to harmonize their roles.

The Founding Fathers gave much thought to the dilemma in its application to the presidency and sought to resolve it through a special means of selection. *The Federalist*, in No. 68, sums up their diagnosis and attempted remedy:

> It was desirable that the sense of the people should operate in the choice of the person to whom so important a trust was to be confided. This end will be answered by committing the right of making it . . . to men chosen by the people for the special purpose, and at the particular conjuncture.
>
> . . . . .
>
> It was also peculiarly desirable to afford as little opportunity as possible to tumult and disorder. . . . The choice of *several*, to form an intermediate body of electors, will be much less apt to convulse the community with any extraordinary or violent movements, than the choice of *one* who was himself to be the final object of the public wishes. . . . [Italics in the original text.]
>
> . . . . .
>
> All these advantages will happily combine in the plan devised by the convention; which is, that the people of each State shall choose a number of persons as electors, equal to the number of senators and representatives of such State in the national government, who shall assemble within the State, and vote for some fit person as President. . . .

. . . . .

The [foregoing] process of election affords a moral certainty, that the office of President will never fall to the lot of any man who is not in an eminent degree endowed with the requisite qualifications. *Talents for low intrigue, and the little arts of popularity, may alone suffice to elevate a man to the first honors in a single State; but it will require other talents, and a different kind of merit, to establish him in the esteem and confidence of the whole Union.* . . . [Italics added.]

The Electoral College still exists, but the vital functions that the Founding Fathers envisaged have long since been drained from it. We have had presidents "in an eminent degree endowed with the requisite qualifications," but we are not in debt to the Electoral College for these happy occasions. Our history reveals some basis for the Founders' apprehension lest "Talents for . . . intrigue, and the . . . arts of popularity, may alone suffice to elevate a man to the first honors in a single State" or county or city. Comparable talents and arts have not usually been unimportant in national conventions that nominate presidents or in elections that pick them.

There may have been times and places in our national history when the disparities were less harmful than they are today. Remedial adjustments may have lain readier to hand, or the damage may have been easier to redeem. At any rate, we may have enjoyed wider margins of tolerance. In the present epoch, the American people sustain and seek to vindicate anew a primary regard for human personality and the values and institutions of freedom. They do so in a world of vast and rapid change, wrenched by dislocations in two world wars and under a recurrent danger of war, stimulated by the opportunities and strained by the tensions of modern science, technology, and industrial organization, and exposed to the threats and blandishments of totalitarian doctrine and practice. In such a world, our margin of tolerance for the discrepancies, if any margin still exists, has narrowed sharply.

The discrepancies have maximum significance when they are felt at the national level because of the preeminent role of the national government, but they are perhaps most striking at the local level. In municipal government, where the problems of racial tensions, educational need and shortcomings, congestion and delay in transportation, urban sprawl, urban blight, and the decay of the central city come to a head, the disparities between the qualities needed to get the job and those needed to do the job at times seem almost grotesque.

I have pointed to the discrepancies as they occur in American government and politics. Are they a distinctively American phenomenon, or is the American case only a particular manifestation of a more general or even universal phenomenon?

I have related the disparities to elections and government in a democracy. Do they grow out of tendencies peculiar to the democratic process, or are they rooted deeper in the nature of political power, however acquired or maintained, and in the functions of government, whatever the form?

In the American experience and the historic experience of other societies, what means have been found to adjust or temper the discrepancies and effect an accommodation between the acquisition of power and the constructive conduct of government?

In the United States today, what can and should be done to extend and deepen such an accommodation?

I will try to illuminate these questions and suggest possible answers to them.

CHAPTER II

SULLA AND CAESAR

. . . the good old rule
Sufficeth them, the simple plan,
That they should take who have the power,
And they should keep who can.

> Wordsworth, "Rob Roy's Grave"

The true forms of government, therefore, are those
in which the one, or the few, or the many, govern
with a view to the common interest; but governments
which rule with a view to the private interest,
whether of the one, or of the few, or of the many,
are perversions. . . . The end of the state is the
good life. . . .

> Aristotle, *Politics* Book III, Chs. 7, 9

In 82 B.C., Lucius Cornelius Sulla entered Rome at the head of his Roman legions, the victor in a civil war and the master of the Roman state.

In 49 B.C., Julius Caesar, descending from Gaul, crossed the Rubicon into Italy and into a far-flung civil war that culminated in his entry into Rome at the head of his legions, the ruler of the Roman state.

Each took power by military force. Each was the champion of a party in bitter political strife, Sulla of the landed senatorial aristocracy, Caesar of the popular party. Sulla was the first Roman general to conclude a political struggle in the Roman republic by the force of Roman arms. Caesar was the last; the republic of Rome died under his rule. The civil war terminated by Sulla's victory was a critical phase, and the civil war ending in Caesar's triumph the climactic phase, of the final century of the Roman republic.

The century 144–44 B.C. began in "a profound calm, scarcely troubled by a ripple here and there on the surface," [1] maintained for a generation after the triumph of Rome over Macedonia in the decisive battle of Pydna in 168 B.C. Carthage had been destroyed thirty-four years earlier. With the subjugation of Macedonia, Rome had extended its sway throughout the Mediterranean area. The calm was shattered by the reforms of the brothers Gracchi, Tiberius and Gaius, and the reaction of the aristocracy. To appraise the significance of the careers of Sulla and Caesar for the present inquiry, we must recall the main elements of the years of tumult and decay between the election of Tiberius Gracchus as tribune of the people in 134 B.C. and the death of Julius Caesar in 44 B.C.

When Tiberius Sempronius Gracchus became a tribune, the principal organs of government of Rome remained essentially as they had been when Rome was a city-state of limited population and extent. The popular assemblies, made up of the entire citizenry meeting as a

[1] Mommsen: *The History of Rome*, ed. Saunders and Collins (New York: Meridian Books, Inc., 1958), 19.

body, had the power under the fundamental law to enact laws and to elect the executive magistrates. The principal executive magistrates were two consuls, elected annually and ranking highest in authority; two censors; eight praetors; a number of quaestors; and the tribunes of the people, a distinctively Roman office. The tribunes were the guardians of popular rights, with a power of veto or intercession against the acts of other magistrates to protect individual citizens or the general populace as a group. The popular assemblies could legislate as they wished and elect anyone they wanted, according to the formal law. In fact, they did nothing of the sort. Under long established usage, when new statutes or decrees were proposed, they were first discussed by the Senate and submitted to the popular assemblies for adoption only if the Senate approved. The executive magistrates (other than the tribunes of the people) were chosen only from the aristocracy, comprising the old landed patricians and a newer nobility deriving their titles from ancestors who had served as consul. In constitutional theory, anyone pleasing to the popular assemblies could still be elected consul and win noble status through the office. In fact, by the middle of the second century B.C., the newer nobility rooted in ancestral office had joined the ancient patrician families rooted in the land to close their ranks and exclude outsiders from the higher magistracies; and the popular assemblies acquiesced. Under the formal law, the Senate, its members also drawn exclusively from the aristocratic class, had power only to advise the executive magistrates on matters of policy; but

12

in practice the executive magistrates regularly sought the Senate's advice and followed it.

The Roman legions drew their manpower primarily from the small farmers who served under a system of compulsory levies. The class of small landholders were long the backbone of the citizenry for civic as well as military purposes. During the wars with Carthage, Hannibal invaded Rome and laid waste the farm lands that had sustained the small landholders; and the long burden of military service during the decades of war with Carthage and Macedonia thinned the numbers of the small farmers, kept them from their fields, and further reduced their livelihood. The Roman victories brought glory to the state and power to the rulers, but not relief to the small farmers. The landowning aristocracy maintained and expanded their position, widening their holdings by occupying public lands. The concentration of landownership in large estates was intensified by the speculative operations of wealthy businessmen of the so-called equestrian order. The fields of the great landowners were worked by slave labor drawn from the ranks of the conquered peoples of Spain, North Africa, Greece, and Asia Minor. The wealthy landowners and businessmen spread their land operations to Sicily and other Mediterranean provinces, producing grain through slave labor at trivial cost. The competition of slave labor in the Italian territory of Rome itself, and of imported grain from provincial fields also worked by slave labor, broke the back of the already overburdened small farming class.

13

By birth and marriage, Tiberius Sempronius Gracchus and his younger brother Gaius derived from impeccable aristocratic antecedents. They were grandsons on their mother's side of Scipio Africanus, the conqueror of Carthage; the father-in-law of Tiberius, Appius Claudius, had served the state as consul and as censor; and Gaius had married the daughter of Publius Crassus Mucianus, who headed the College of Priests as *pontifex maximus*. Sensing the peril to Rome that germinated in the decay of the class of small landholders, Tiberius aspired to conserve the vitality of the state by regenerating the class.

On taking office as tribune, he undertook to revive and strengthen the substance of an ancient agrarian law that had lain as a dead letter for over two centuries. His proposal contemplated repossession by the state of public lands that had drifted into the hands of large landowners who had occupied them originally without any payment to the state. Each occupier would be permitted to retain 500 acres for himself and 250 acres for each of his sons up to an aggregate maximum of 1,000 acres; and some provision appears to have been made to compensate the occupiers for buildings they might have erected and other improvements. The heart of the reform lay in the plan for disposition of the land repossessed. It would be divided into plots of 30 acres to be distributed to citizens willing to commit themselves to farm the plots and pay a modest rental to the state. Mindful of the lapse of the old law for lack of administration, Tiberius put the teeth of enforcement into the planned new measure. He proposed a commission of three magistrates, to be elected each

14

year by the popular assembly, charged with the duty of advancing the law from the books into action.

The Senate resisted, and enlisted the support of another tribune of the people. Blocked by a veto interposed by his fellow tribune, Tiberius broke the ancient custom under which new legislation was submitted to the popular assemblies only after prior approval by the Senate. Appearing before the assembly, he called for the removal of the rival tribune and enactment of the new measure. The multitude responded in joyous assent. They voted to unseat the obstinate tribune, adopted the agrarian reform, and accepted the nomination of Tiberius himself, his brother Gaius, and his father-in-law, Appius Claudius, as the three members of the land commission.

While the proposal to repossess lands long held by members of the large landowning class had provoked resentment enough among the aristocracy, a minority could understand the need and sympathize with the purpose. But Tiberius' direct appeal to the power of the popular assemblies latent in the letter of the formal law, in defiance of the usage subordinating the popular assemblies in practice to the Senate, inflamed the hostility of the majority of the aristocracy and transformed the issues for the minority. The aristocracy drew together in anger and foreboding.

It may be doubted how far Tiberius appreciated the revolutionary implications of his act, at least in the first instance, or whether he foresaw the chain of consequences. He was not permitted to live long enough for his first impressions to be ripened by experience. The fears of the Senate boiled up into an outbreak of fury shortly after his victory in the popular assembly. When the popular assembly met again to elect tribunes for the year 133 B.C., its session was shattered by an invasion of senators armed with chair legs wrenched from the furniture of the Senate. They pursued Tiberius Gracchus and bludgeoned him to death.

During a brief remission of temper and hate that followed, cooler heads in the Senate managed to prevail to some degree. The agrarian law was permitted to remain on the books, and the land commission was even allowed to make a beginning toward the exercise of its duties. But the deeper issues persisted, and the forces stirred up by Tiberius drove and were manipulated by his younger brother and successor.

Gaius Sempronius Gracchus, elected tribune of the people in his turn, for political reasons of his own brought about an enactment that every citizen of Rome who presented himself in the capital would receive a monthly allotment of grain from public stores at nominal prices. Drawn by the prospect of free grain, the pauperized small farmers drifted to the capital within which the distribution was confined. Others left their fields for service in the army in the provinces or along the borders of the Roman domain, attracted by the prospect of military booty. In Rome itself, the multitude of citizens on the dole was augmented by freed slaves and subjects from the provinces, of diverse races and creeds, attracted to Rome by the lure of free sustenance and the glamour of the capital.

Gradually replacing the small farmer citizenry in the

16

popular assemblies, the rootless and destitute urban rabble became an instrument of politics and a political force. The assemblies deteriorated in their composition while their powers increased and duties multiplied as a by-product of the expansion of Rome. Originally constituting the electorate and the lawmaking organ of a small and homogeneous city-state, the popular assemblies at the time of the Gracchi found themselves the lawmaking organ (according to the formal law) and the electorate of a vast and varied population and territory.

The transformation of the civil society was paralleled by a change in the army. The progressive displacement of free farmers by slaves in the countryside diminished the manpower available for the traditional levies. The uprooted small farmers who chose the army as an avenue out of their distress served for pay and the opportunities for pillage. Deprived of land and a civic status to which they could return, they became mercenary troops without a sense of place in the structure of the civil society or the state. The members of the urban rabble who were enrolled in the legions served in a similar mood. The military governors and generals in the outlying provinces supplemented the Roman numbers with soldiers enlisted from the conquered peoples, who served under compulsion or for pay or loot, without any sense of attachment or commitment to the Roman state. The Roman legions were converted from citizen soldiers, for whom military duties and civic duties were different aspects of a single responsibility of citizenship in a state with which they identified themselves and their families, to professional

17

troops without civic connections to the Roman state, tied only to their commanders, their comrades in arms, and their own interests.

The transformations were marked by deepening hostility among the aristocracy, the merchants and investors of the equestrian order, and the proletariat. The Senate's actual sphere of influence and power and the power of the aristocracy wielded through the Senate had rested upon long acquiescence crystallized into custom. The sanctions of custom, initially broken by Tiberius Gracchus, tended to dissolve in the pervasive bitterness among the classes, and the position of the Senate became vulnerable to the assaults of popular leaders backed by the power of the rabble making up the popular assemblies which the leaders could manipulate. The agrarian reforms of Tiberius and Gaius Gracchus and their attacks upon the citadels of the aristocracy marked the beginning of a long process of dissolution.

The senatorial aristocracy and the mercantile class reacted, and counterattacked in their turn. The murder of Tiberius Gracchus and the despairing suicide of Gaius yielded only an interlude of quiet. As the intermittent struggle dragged on, it became more virulent and the methods and measures employed more violent. It burst into civil war in 88 B.C. Arrested by Sulla's first victory, the struggle erupted again when Sulla withdrew his armies for a campaign in Asia Minor. The popular party won ascendancy under its leaders Marius and Cinna, who gave vent to their spleen in a massacre of their opponents. The senatorial party clamored for Sulla. As soon as conditions in the field permitted, Sulla returned at the head of his troops and restored the dominance of the aristocracy under his personal rule.

Sulla restored the power of the Senate and the ascendancy of the aristocratic class. He crushed the opposition and killed its leaders. To consolidate his position and the status of the aristocracy, he embarked upon a program of massacre and confiscation that made his name a synonym for terror and proscription in succeeding centuries. He carried out his program with cold and systematic rigor, methodically compiling lists of names to be proscribed and publishing them, setting bounties on their heads, and duly entering the rewards paid to killers in the public books of account. His measures were effective. Not a whisper of resistance persisted.

Sulla executed his program through the same troops and commanders that had carried him to victory. Was his then a case that refutes the thesis put forward in the previous chapter? Did he acquire power through one kind of man and govern through the same kind of man?

The questions point to ambiguities in the concept of government. A raw view could be taken that would equate the acquisition, maintenance, and exercise of power with the conduct of government. Under such a view, pirates who capture a port or brigands who overrun a countryside would be deemed to govern. To get power, to keep it, and to use it for the advantage or whim of those in power would be the whole of the matter.

In the total history of mankind as a species on the face of the earth, such a view has perhaps been vindicated as

19

often as not by the behavior of men in power. Gibbon, contemplating the story of Rome from the perspective of the eighteenth century, wrote of the emperors Antoninus Pius and Marcus Aurelius Antoninus: "Their united reigns are possibly the only period of history in which the happiness of a great people was the sole object of government." [2] Gibbon published his observation on February 1, 1776, four months and four days before the proclamation of the Declaration of Independence. To the authors of the Declaration, it was self-evident that "all men . . . are endowed by their Creator with certain unalienable Rights, that among these are Life, Liberty and the Pursuit of Happiness.—That to secure these rights, Governments are instituted among Men, ..." Eleven years later, the Founding Fathers were more explicit in declaring the purposes of the government which they had constituted: ". . . to form a more perfect Union, establish Justice, insure domestic Tranquility, provide for the common defence, promote the general Welfare, and secure the Blessings of Liberty to ourselves and our Posterity . . . ." Spokesmen for other societies would state their aims differently; but the consensus of the twentieth century would affirm that government consists of far more than the getting, keeping, and exercise of power.

Sulla might have undertaken to secure the position of the senatorial aristocracy by restoring the foundations of the republic. He might have tried to shore up the sagging

[2] Gibbon: *The Dicline and Fall of the Roman Empire,* ed. Bury (London: Methuen & Co.; 1909), I, 84.

main beam of the structure, the condition of the small farmers. He might have tried to clean out or contain the rot of slavery. None should have been more aware than he of the danger to the political order from the newly arisen mercenary armies, bound only to their commanders and themselves, feeling no allegiance to the Roman state. He might have tried to reconstitute the armed forces or establish countervailing safeguards. He might have tried to readjust the ancient institutions of the republic to the new scale and variety of its existence. He never made any such attempt. To have done so, he would have required resources of understanding and skill lacking in his troops and subordinate commanders and the vengeful aristocrats through whom he executed his measures of retaliation and suppression. ". . . [He] succeeded in creating, not a Constitution or an Empire, but simply a gigantic system of police—conceived with unerring clearness, and executed with superhuman energy. . . ."[3] Only because he undertook no more did the men through whom he acquired power seem adequate to the administration of his office. Possibly Ferrero was extreme in his estimate that "Sulla contributed nothing at all."[4] Sulla's rule may not have been entirely devoid of substantive content. Perhaps he did for a time cement the relations between Rome and her Italian allies. Perhaps he contributed a marginal point or two to the development of Roman criminal procedure.

[3] Ferrero: *The Greatness and Decline of Rome,* tr. Zimmern (New York: G. P. Putnam's Sons; 1909), I, 116.
[4] Ibid., p. 117.

Yet in essence Sulla dominated, but did not govern.

A little more than three decades later, Julius Caesar, as the leader of the popular party but relying on the power of his own legions, won a larger civil war that raged in Italy and throughout the Roman dominions, and established his personal rule. When he came to power, the processes of degeneration in the life of the Roman republic had run their course for an additional thirty-three years. The civil wars of Sulla had been confined to Italy, but the wars which led to the victory of Caesar ravaged the provinces as well as the metropolis. The mutual hatred among the classes had become even sharper; the infestation of slavery had spread even wider; the irresponsibility of the Roman proletariat and the provincial generals and mercenary armies had become even more mischievous. Caesar won ascendancy through the power of his legions and with the acclaim of demagogues and a proletariat no less angry and implacable than the aristocrats of Sulla's day.

Caesar had no desire to restore the Republic; nor did he want to slake the passion of his followers, the greed of his troops or his personal ambition in a naked exercise of punishment and domination. He burned with ambition of a more complex sort. He relished the game of power and its pleasures, but he wanted also to found an empire that would endure and command the regard of peoples and generations. For these ends, Caesar recognized the inadequacy of the men through whom he had won power. He wasted no time in trying to carry out his purposes through them alone.

22

Aware of his need for other men, he sought them throughout the society, and found them largely among the opponents he had vanquished. To use them, he had to master the hatred of the opposition and the resentment of his following.

Repudiating the tradition bequeathed to the popular party by Marius and Cinna, he held political reprisals to a minimum. He permitted many who had been banished to return from exile, and restored civic rights to many who had lost them through attainder. An amnesty granted to the common soldiers of the armies that had fought against him was in time extended by specific exceptions or general decrees to many of the officers. Caesar's own adherents of the popular party gnashed their teeth over the denial of the feast of vengeance which they had anticipated. Here and there, they got out of hand, and broke loose in street riots. They were quickly suppressed.

Caesar sought to forestall an increase in the uprooted urban rabble from the ranks of the idle troops. Within Italy itself, he earmarked much public land for distribution to small farmers, giving preference to his own veteran troops. In an effort to prevent the new farms from slipping into the hands of rich speculators, he made them unsaleable for twenty years after the grant by the state to the initial recipients. Embarking upon a program of overseas colonization, he managed to transplant some eighty thousand persons to new lives as colonists in the Roman dominions. Where he could, he proceeded through incentives, such as the opening of colonial senates to the candidacies of freed men. In the main, he

23

seems to have effected the colonization by command.

Mommsen in his analysis sought to expose the essence of Caesar's political method:

Caesar's high purposes required the constitutional party itself, which in fact embraced not only the aristocracy but all the elements of a free national spirit among the Italian citizenry. His schemes, which sought to renovate the antiquated state, needed the whole mass of talent, culture, and hereditary and self-acquired distinction comprehended within this party, and in this sense he may well have regarded the pardoning of his opponents as the finest reward of victory. Accordingly the most prominent chiefs were indeed removed, but full pardon was not withheld from men of the second and third rank, especially younger men. These were not, moreover, allowed to sulk in passive opposition, but by more or less gentle pressure were made to take an active part in the new administration and to accept honors and offices from it.

. . . . .

. . . By . . . not simply sparing the partisans but allowing every man of talent . . . to hold office regardless of his political past, he focused on his great design the massed energies of the state; and the voluntary or compulsory participation of men of all parties in the same work imperceptibly led the nation over to the newly prepared ground. Nor was he misled by the fact that this reconciliation was for the moment only external, and that there was much less agreement about the new state of things than about hatred for Caesar. He knew well that antagonisms lose their keenness when brought into outward union, and that only thus can the statesman assist the working of time, which alone can heal such strife by laying the old generation in the grave. . . .[5]

Other historians of Rome have been less ardent than Mommsen in their admiration for Caesar. Examining the record half a century later than the German historian, Guglielmo Ferrero discerned many of the same ingredients but a different essence. In Ferrero's view, the triumphant Caesar was "not in the least interested in the constitutional question that was absorbing so the leisured classes at Rome; his sole and all-engrossing thought was . . . the annexation of Parthia." [6] Tired out from his efforts in the civil war and from recurrent attacks of epilepsy, he was stirred to new exertions more by a vision of conquest in Parthia than by a dream of regeneration in Rome. His plan to extend the empire and find new sources of revenue in the East shaped his course. "Every day Rome was stupefied to hear of some new and daring project. The Dictator intended to divert the course of the Tiber in order to drain the Pontine marshes; . . . to establish large libraries in all parts of Rome; to pierce the Isthmus of Corinth; . . . to create a huge port at Ostia; . . . to collect and codify all the existing laws: all schemes to be executed, of course, after the completion of the great Parthian campaign. . . ." [7] The scope and

[5] *The History of Rome,* pp. 493, 494–5.
[6] *The Greatness and Decline of Rome,* II, 327.
[7] Ibid., pp. 328–9.

form of the powers he assumed were determined by his needs for the prospective campaign as well as his habit of seizing opportunities as they arose. The same needs largely dictated his policy of leniency toward his political opponents and amnesty for many of the officers and troops whom he had defeated in the civil war. He had "to assume the fullest possible powers, yet to set out [on his campaign] without leaving too many enemies behind his back. He needed, if he could, to have a favourable public." [8]

While endorsing Mommsen's acclaim of Caesar as " 'a great orator, a great writer, and a great general,' " Ferrero rejected Mommsen's crowning tribute that Caesar " 'became all these because he was an incomparable statesman.' " [9] Ferrero also disputed a common assessment by historians "that, because Caesar had been able to construct so wonderful an instrument of rule as his army, he was thereby placed in a position where he could govern and reorganize the Empire as he wished." The common assessment, Ferrero insisted, missed the point. Caesar "had indeed used his army as an incomparable weapon of destruction; it had helped him to crush the Conservative party and destroy the legitimate government; but it could not help him . . . to form a new government on the ruins of the old. . . . He stood alone, and well-nigh helpless, in the place of power." [1]

To Ferrero, "Caesar was not a great statesman; but he was a great destroyer." This was the heart of the matter. "For we fail to grasp the true significance of Caesar's career till we discern that . . . his mission was prima-

[8] Ibid., p. 334.   [9] Ibid., p. 344 n.   [1] Ibid., p. 311.

rily destructive—to complete the disorganization and dissolution of the old world, both in Italy and the provinces. . . ." Despite Caesar's "Protean genius," his victory in the civil war left him "suspended between two equally impossible alternatives—either to abandon the position he had just triumphantly captured, or, almost single-handed, with the help of a few personal adherents, to administer a huge and disorganised Empire." The tides of dissolution ran too strongly to permit the rebuilding of Roman society out of the debris. "The times called for a quieter, a more cautious, a more patient race of workers. . . . death rescued . . . Caesar from an entanglement which not even he could have unravelled. . . ." [2]

If we accept Mommsen's appreciation, Caesar was doubly gifted with the arts of acquiring power and the arts of governing. He achieved political ascendancy through the use of men of one sort; he governed largely through men of a different kind.

If we follow Ferrero's analysis, Caesar had the qualities to win power; but at his time of supreme power, he was too tangled in a mesh of habit, illness, fatigue, and passions born of the spirit of the times to be able to turn to governing. He attained power through attributes and men of one kind; he did not find within himself the attributes of another kind nor in Rome the men of another kind needed to govern.

By either appraisal, Caesar's experience, like Sulla's, reveals the discrepancy between the qualities and sort of men needed to win power and those required to govern.

[2] Ibid., pp. 345, 346, 355.

CHAPTER III

THE FRENCH REVOLUTION
AND NAPOLEON

The government of the Republic is vested in an
Emperor, who will assume the title of Emperor
of the French.

Constitution of the Year XII of
the French Revolution (May 18, 1804)

When Napoleon seized control in France in the guise of
First Consul, he was not unmindful of possible similarities
to Julius Caesar. "In the first place France required a
strong government. While I was at the head of it, I may
say that France was in the same condition as Rome when
a dictator was declared necessary for the salvation of the
Republic." [1]

Napoleon's life spanned a great divide in the history of
the West, raised by the coinciding forces of the French
Revolution, the American Revolution and the Industrial
Revolution. Beyond the divide, science, technology,
spreading popular participation in government and a
political vision of human rights derived from a religious-

---

[1] Napoleon to O'Meara, quoted in *The Cambridge Modern
History,* IX, 763.

philosophical concept of the dignity of man transformed the conditions in which men came to power and governed. The conditions in which Napoleon won supremacy in France were formed by the first ten years of the French Revolution. The Revolution ran its remaining course in circumstances shaped by Napoleon's pursuit of an expanded dominion and by his conduct of government.

The Declaration of the Rights of Man was proclaimed on August 26, 1789, by the National Constituent Assembly, the first in a kaleidoscopic series of governing bodies created and destroyed by the French Revolution. The Declaration not only formulated the list of rights for which it is famous, but defined the aim of government as "the preservation of the natural and imprescriptible rights of man," much as the American Declaration of Independence had done thirteen years earlier. The principal author of the American Declaration witnessed the French events from close at hand. Two days after the National Constituent Assembly had acted, Thomas Jefferson, then the American Minister to France, wrote from Paris to James Madison: ". . . Their declaration of rights is finished. If printed in time I will inclose a copy with this." Jefferson rejoiced in the accomplishment and in the good will of the Assembly toward the United States whose "proceedings have been viewed as a model for them on every occasion; and tho in the heat of debate men are generally disposed to contradict every authority urged by their opponents, ours has been treated like that of the bible, open to explanation but not to question." But he added a note of misgiving: "The distress for money endangers everything. No taxes are payed, and no money can be borrowed." [2]

The National Constituent Assembly inherited empty coffers from the old regime. Earlier in the year, Louis XVI's financial distress had impelled him to convene the Estates General, the ancient representative congress of France, for the first time since 1614. Brittle from long disuse, the Estates General had split in a tug of war among its components, the representatives of the nobility, those of the clergy, and those of the "third estate," roughly corresponding in social composition to the more highly evolved commons of England. The last broke away and reassembled on their own under the name of the National Assembly, vowing to remain in session until they could form a new constitution for the realm. They were joined by many of the clergy and a few nobles; but the king and the bulk of the nobility resisted. The ensuing struggle between them was soon absorbed in a wider upheaval.

The pent-up grievances and hopes of the populace erupted in the storming of the Bastille on July 14, 1789, and peasant risings throughout the provinces. Successive waves of revolution engulfed the monarchy; washed away more and more of the existing social order; displaced the National Assembly by the Convention; concentrated the power of the Convention in the Committee of Public Safety; and rose to a peak of fury in the Reign of Terror. From 1792 on, the internal revolution was accom-

[2] Letter of August 28, 1789, in *Works of Thomas Jefferson*, ed. P. L. Ford (New York: G. P. Putnam's Sons; 1904), V, 487, 488, 491.

panied by almost incessant external war against shifting coalitions of hostile states, variously made up of Austria, Prussia, Holland, Spain, Russia, the Italian states, the Ottoman Empire, and France's most formidable enemy of the time, Great Britain.

The successive revolutionary regimes could muster power to abolish the aristocracy, kill or exile internal foes of the revolution and wage victorious war against foreign enemies. They could not master or manage their own following enough to maintain internal order, install a competent administration, collect taxes, or borrow money.

Under the mounting demands of revolution and war, the financial stringency bequeathed to the revolution by the old regime went from acute to desperate. The governing bodies resorted to confiscation and to the printing press. They seized the lands of the clergy, the Crown, and the exiled or refugee nobility, and issued paper money— *assignats* and *mandats*—ostensibly backed by the value of the enlarged public domain. The want of internal order, administration, and fiscal and financial institutions doomed the new currency. It collapsed in a familiar pattern of expanding volume and contracting value. An original issue of *assignats* in a face amount of four hundred millions multiplied in a few years to a face amount of forty-five billions. The value of the units dropped toward the vanishing point.

In an unceasing contest for supremacy among revolutionary factions, a moderate group gained the upper hand in 1795. Under their sway, the governing body of

THE THINGS THAT ARE CAESAR'S

the time, the Convention, recaptured for itself as a whole
the power which it had been forced to delegate to a
Committee of Public Safety and the Committee's leader,
Robespierre. Robespierre followed his long line of victims
to the guillotine; and the Reign of Terror ground to a
halt, its concentrated violence dissipated into the more
general disorder. A new constitution was proclaimed, the
third of the revolution, and the Convention gave way to
the Directory. In the transition, the revolutionary regime
was challenged in a backlash of royalist resentment.
The outbreak is remembered chiefly for the "whiff of
grapeshot" that suppressed it, from guns under the
command of a young artillery officer to whom the Convention had assigned its troops, Napoleon Bonaparte.

Externally, the success of the French revolutionary
armies continued to astonish the world. In 1795, France
overran Belgium, invaded Holland, and took Flanders by
conquest. Prussia, Saxony, Hanover, and Hesse-Cassel
were forced to sue for peace on France's terms, Prussia
consenting to the absolute cession of the left bank of the
Rhine to France. Spain also was glad to sign a treaty of
peace. The revolution could handle its avowed enemies,
foreign and royalist. It could not master its own partisans
nor meet its needs at home.

The contrast between external vigor and internal mismanagement persisted under the Directory as under its
predecessors. The treasury remained empty and the
currency valueless, despite a solemn burning of the
plates upon which the *assignats* had been printed. The
ritual of cremation failed to exorcise the evil spirits.

Other plates were made and worthless *mandats* replaced the repudiated *assignats*. The civil employees of the regime were largely unpaid and its soldiers often went without shoes. Bread riots broke out. At its wits' ends, the Directory embraced a plan put forward by the officer whose guns had fired the "whiff of grape shot" in the Tuileries.

Bonaparte proposed to convert the fortunes of war into a remedy for bankruptcy. He would extend the war to the "rich provinces" of Italy where he would find "honor, glory and riches." [3] Entrusted with the desired command, Bonaparte moved down along the coast to Nice, defeating the Austrians and the Piedmontese. After forcing the cession of Savoy and Nice to France, he moved on to Milan and Mantua, conquered Lombardy, and threatened Rome. The Pope, in the capacity of a temporal ruler, hastened to eliminate the threat by a treaty of peace with Napoleon in which Romagna, Bologna, and Ferrara were added to the roster of captured territories. The spoils of Bonaparte's Italian victories met the costs of the Italian campaign and provided a surplus for the harassed Directory.

Napoleon had devised a formula for financing his campaigns with the fruits of victory which he was to exploit for fifteen years of war and conquest. At home, the combination of military glory and financial relief secured Bonaparte's reputation and enhanced his popularity.

[3] Quoted in Bainville: *Histoire de France* (Paris: Librairie Arthème Fayard; 1961), p. 379.

The respite for the Directory was brief. The interacting afflictions of insolvency, factional struggle, economic dislocation, and social disorder soon resumed their course. The prolonged wars, even when victorious, took their toll in popular fatigue and disaffection, and the sequence of victories did not continue unbroken. In 1799, under the pressure of a new coalition against France formed initially between Great Britain and Russia and joined by Austria, the Ottoman Empire, Portugal, and the Kingdom of Naples, the fortunes of war turned against France.

Bonaparte had invaded Egypt in a campaign designed to bring Britain down by striking at her Indian empire. The British Navy destroyed the French fleet at Aboukir, stranding Napoleon and his forces along the Nile. Reverses dislodged French armies that had been living off the land in subjugated areas of Italy, Germany, and Switzerland. Driven back into France, the French troops, tired and hungry, turned their practice of requisition against the towns and countryside of France. The intensified disorder produced a spasm of revulsion among the populace and troops and demoralized the government itself.

In Egypt, Napoleon heard reports of the spreading dsintegration in France and sensed the opportunity offered to an energetic general popular among the men of the revolution. He slipped out of Egypt, eluded the British blockade, and landed on the French coast.

He was greeted in a frenzy of relief by crowds crying "*Vive la République*," and made his way across France to the capital in a triumphant procession. On November 9, 1799, the "18 Brumaire" of the revolutionary calendar, the Directory fell. The event is customarily described as a *coup d'état* led by Napoleon. It could be described just as well as an abdication of the Directory in favor of Napoleon. The "18 Brumaire" was organized inside the government by two of the directors, Siéyès and Roger-Duclos, assisted by Napoleon's brother, Lucien Bonaparte, then president of a council organized under the Directory, the Council of Five Hundred. Napoleon climbed to power on the shoulders of the politicians of the revolution as well as his own grenadiers.

The Directory was superseded by the Consulate, a regime of transition between the republic that it ended and the empire into which it evolved. Bonaparte, as First Consul, dominated the Consulate. He had come, according to the often quoted dictum of Thiers, "to continue the revolution in the world under monarchical forms."

Swiftly Napoleon extended and tightened his grip. Initially First Consul for a term of ten years under the Constitution of 1799, he had himself made Consul for life in 1802. Two years later, the form of government was again changed to conform to the facts of Napoleon's rule. The Consulate gave way to the Empire, and Napoleon became the Emperor of France. In one sense, he had reached the pinnacle of power. In another sense, he remained a climber on the heights of power until his eventual collapse. His appetite was boundless, and however great the reach of his dominion, he wanted always to stretch it. But the mere possession and exercise of power, whatever its extent, could not satisfy him. He craved the excitement of accomplishment through the use of power, and sought to enshrine his name in institutional monuments as well as monuments of stone. He wanted to impress himself indelibly upon the structure of France through innovations identified with him that would endure. To that end, he undertook to give France a "system of government . . . adapted to the national temperament and to circumstances." [4]

When Napoleon turned from the acquisition of power to the conduct of government, he turned away from the politicians and generals who helped elevate him to power. He sought and found other men.

Initially, the politicians of the Directory who had aided in the *coup d'état* did move on with Napoleon into the regime of the Consulate. They largely manned the Senate, the Legislative Body, and the Tribunate, the three principal organs other than the Consuls established by the Constitution of 1799. But Napoleon rapidly drained power from the other organs to himself as First Consul, and surrounded himself by new men, Councilors of State and the heads of a newly established bureaucracy.

The generals were no happier than the Directory politicians at the rapid concentration of power in Napoleon's hands and his elaboration of a structure of government through other men. The officers of the revolutionary army were mainly children of the revolution. Although the Consulate and the Empire in action did

[4] Napoleon to O'Meara, quoted in *The Cambridge Modern History*, IX, 763.

little to vindicate the Declaration of the Rights of Man, some of the spirit of the Declaration and fervor of the early revolution remained alive in many minds and hearts, in the army as well as in the populace. Napoleon recognized the condition and its possible consequences. When the treaties of Lunéville and Florence in 1801 and the Treaty of Amiens early in 1802 brought peace to all of Europe—for what proved to be a short interlude—he took steps to forestall action to which idle military hands might be tempted. He selected regiments noted for their revolutionary zeal and assigned them to San Domingo.

In a corner of his mind, he may also have toyed with another purpose. Hungry for dominion over more than the Old World, he may have transferred the troops in part to anticipate a possible use of San Domingo as an eventual staging area for a possible attempt to restore the empire of France in the Western Hemisphere. But his immediate motive was to remove the regiments from political temptation.

Additional measures proved to be necessary. A number of senior officers, released from active duty by the treaties of peace, gathered in the capital. There they had opportunities to observe and time to reflect; and republican principles, personal disappointment, jealousy, and pique could work freely upon them. They became uneasy. In Bernadotte, Moreau, Masséna, and ten or eleven others, anxiety hardened into hostility. Pamphlets secretly distributed by Bernadotte's chief of staff warned: "Soldiers, you have no longer a country; the Republic has ceased to exist. A tyrant has seized upon power; and that tyrant is

Bonaparte." [5] Alerted by his police, Napoleon sought to pull the teeth of the conspiracy by a declaration before the Council of State remarkable for its irony: "Never will military government take root in France unless the nation has first been brutalised by fifty years of ignorance." [6] In due course, the conspirators were arrested. Whether out of contempt or political tactics, Napoleon disposed of them gently and without publicity. He dismissed a few from the service and removed the others to a safe distance by dispatching them to embassies and missions far from France.

Napoleon's method of governing and choice of men are exemplified in the Council of State, the regional and local administration, and the rehabilitation of the public finances.

The Constitution of 1799 had provided for a Council of State but left its organization indeterminate. Napoleon defined its structure in an ordinance and appointed its members. He made the Council his chosen instrument and increased its functions year by year. It met daily, either as a whole or in one or another of five sections into which it was organized. It assisted in legislation by preparing drafts of statutes and decrees; it advised Napoleon and the heads of the bureaucracy on the interpretation of laws; it served as a judicial tribunal to give redress against alleged administrative abuses; and it performed a variety of staff and administrative duties.

The regional and local administration of France was

[5] Quoted in *The Cambridge Modern History*, IX, 21.
[6] Ibid.

centralized through an organizational hierarchy culminating in the First Consul, later the Emperor. Subprefects administered districts, reporting to prefects who administered departments embracing the districts; and the prefects reported to the heads of the bureaucracy in Paris, tightly reined by Napoleon.

Like his predecessors in the succession of revolutionary governments, Napoleon faced an empty treasury at the threshold of his regime. Unlike his predecessors, he managed to fill it. At long last, he put an end to the fiscal and monetary ineptitude and confusion that had plagued Louis XVI, the National Assembly, the Legislative Assembly, the Convention, and the Directory. Responsibility for the collection of taxes in each district was concentrated in a collector, answering to a superior collector charged with similar responsibility for each department. The latter reported back through channels to the Ministry of Finance. Closely controlled and energetically driven, taking advantage of Napoleon's authority and popularity and growing public confidence in the stability of his rule, the new administration effectively collected current taxes and cut into the immense arrearages left by prior incompetence. The reform in taxation was accompanied by a consolidation of the public debt, a reform of the currency and the establishment of a Bank of France.

In the appointment of councilors of state, ministers, heads of bureaus, prefects, and collectors, Napoleon prescribed and enforced criteria of selection that ignored social origin and political affiliation. He looked to intelligence, energy, industry, and disciplined obedience. These qualities established, he cared little whether a man had been a Jacobin or a servant of the monarchy, a member of a revolutionary assembly or an officer of the army. He recruited from the ranks of the unknown as well as the ranks of the known.

His practice can be illustrated in two critical and sensitive sectors of his government, the reorganization of the public finances and the reform of the legal system. The reconstitution of the fiscal and monetary system owed much to the Minister of Finance, Gaudin. Gaudin had served as a civil servant under the monarchy for some fourteen years prior to the revolution. In the preparation of the Code Napoleon, the civil code that represents perhaps the most durable and influential achievement of Napoleon's regime, initial responsibility was assigned to a committee of four lawyers. The dominant impulse in the preparatory committee came from Tronchet and Portalis. Tronchet, the "Nestor of the aristocracy," had been of counsel for the defense along with two colleagues in the trial of Louis XVI that ended in the execution of the king in January, 1793. He had long served as president of the Court of Cassation. Portalis had served as an assessor in Provence under the monarchy. Imprisoned in 1793 under the Republic and subsequently released, he had become a leader of a party of moderates opposed to the Directory. He had been proscribed and had fled to Switzerland, where he had lived in exile until the accession of Bonaparte as First Consul.

In sum, Napoleon took power with men of one sort but governed largely through another sort. The record shows it. We also have his own word for it. As a prisoner on St. Helena, he had abundant leisure to review the course he had run. He described it as he wanted posterity to see it, in his formal memoirs and informal reminiscences recorded by one or another of the companions allowed him by his captors. Dr. Barry O'Meara, the surgeon of the British cruiser *Bellerophon* on which Napoleon had first been taken into custody, had been assigned to duty as the royal prisoner's medical attendant at the prisoner's request. In a conversation with O'Meara on St. Helena, Napoleon compressed his doctrine for appointments in government into the famous phrase: *"La carrière ouverte aux talents."* [7]

Napoleon's reminiscences were self-serving, of course. But even with a cautionary measure of salt, his slogan can be swallowed without gagging. It is supported by the evidence, which also reveals a second level of meaning. In the usual acceptation, the slogan is taken to proclaim a democratic equality of opportunity and selection on the merits. Although accurate as far as it goes, the customary understanding is incomplete. As the record discloses, the slogan also meant appointment on the basis of talents needed to govern, rather than prior usefulness in winning power.

[7] "The career open to talents," quoted in O'Meara, *Napoleon in Exile*.

CHAPTER IV

THE CONGO

Pioneer angels cleared the way
For a Congo paradise, for babes at play,
For sacred capitals, for temples clean.
Gone were the skull-faced witch-men lean. . . .

Vachel Lindsay, "The Congo"

The Republic of the Congo came into being on July 1, 1960. Its boundaries, defined not by African ethnic or cultural history but by European conquest, embraced the land and tribes previously governed by Belgium as the Belgian Congo. It emerged as part of a process that converted Africa from a passive vessel for European expansion into a continent of African states, resolved to pursue their destinies in their own way.

At the end of World War II, the world's roster of states that could be called independent included only four in Africa: Egypt, Ethiopia, Liberia, and the Union of South Africa. Twenty-five additional African states appeared within the next fifteen years, nineteen in 1960 and 1961 alone. By the beginning of 1964, thirty-five of the 113 member states of the United Nations were African, more than 30 per cent of the total.

The birth pangs of the new states were felt in the

42

United Nations. The Thirteenth General Assembly in 1958–59 was dubbed the "African session," and the preoccupation of the "African session" with African states was fully matched two years later in the Fifteenth General Assembly. The Fifteenth dealt with Africa as a whole and with many parts; it admitted sixteen African states to United Nations membership; and it heard a five-point program for Africa proposed by the President of the United States in an address outlining a comprehensive United States policy toward the continent. The General Assembly's anxieties at the Fifteenth session were focused upon the newborn Republic of the Congo.

The self-assertion of Africa is part of a world-wide process, comprising the emergence of new independent states and the modernization of underdeveloped societies. The drive to reach nationhood and independence and the drive to modernize are distinct impulses, but they have been so closely associated in their occurrence and consequences that they may be regarded as aspects of a single phenomenon. The phenomenon has rivaled the confrontation between the free and the Communist societies and the advent of nuclear energy as a paramount factor in international affairs since the end of World War II. It has been the dominant factor in the internal political life of much of Latin America, Asia, and the Pacific islands, as well as Africa.

To the peoples involved, independence means freedom from a former colonial yoke. By a psychological extension, it also means freedom from any suspicion of control by another state, especially the kind of state which in their historic experience has wielded colonial power. Modernization means in essence the incorporation into the society of modern science, technology, and industrial organization. While the twin drives to establish independent states and to modernize underdeveloped societies reached a peak of intensity in the aftermath of World War II, their origins can be traced back to the expansion of Europe and to the Industrial Revolution, the French Revolution, and the American Revolution.

The science and technology that transformed Europe and North America spread to the other continents along the highways of exploration, trade, conquest, and colonization. So did the ideas proclaimed in the Declaration of Independence and the Declaration of the Rights of Man. As the strength of the West reduced areas to a colonial condition or other forms of dependence, the culture of the West planted seeds in those areas that sprouted ultimately in aspirations toward self-fulfillment and a will to emulate Western productivity and power. Lumumba and Kasavubu in the Republic of the Congo in 1960 were would-be heirs, presumably unknowing, of Jefferson and Danton as well as of unnumbered scientists and inventors of whom they had never heard. Yet, as they discovered, a claim to a heritage and even its allowance do not automatically lead to an enjoyment of its benefits. There must be an understanding of the heritage and a capacity to put it to use. With so complex an inheritance received in the newly developing states through so intricate a channel of transmittal, the obstacles to use are multiplied, and there are side-effects. The difficulties are felt at many points and in many ways, not least in the relationship between political power and the conduct of government.

Science, its application in technology, and the application of both science and technology in economic organization provide instruments that can be used to take power in a state, extend its reach, and fortify its grip. To men desiring only to get power and keep it, the results of science and technology can be sweet. When they undertake to govern, they encounter consequences of quite another sort. Science and its applications complicate a society, making it harder to understand and to manage. At the same time, they heighten popular expectations. Impressed by the productivity of modern science, technology, and industrial organization, the citizenry insist upon the fruits. They want their share. They become impatient with delay. In prior centuries, people often found it hard to believe what science could do. In the twentieth century, people are often unable or unwilling to recognize that there are limits to what science can do. They tend to regard even apparent limits as provisional, for again and again they have seen science magnify its power by exercising it. Even in the modern industrial states, and especially in the newly developing societies, there is a widespread tendency to believe that the means are at last at hand to fill the age-old wants of men. The populace demands of governments that the wants be met. In the emerging states, the job of government thus becomes enlarged and complicated at the very time when the new men first take it up. The transition from taking power to governing becomes correspondingly rough. The Republic of the Congo is an illuminating case.

The Congo experience exemplifies a general pattern in the new modernizing states despite its extraordinary intensity. Although it lies at one extreme within a range of typical cases, it is not a special case. Its fire highlights the elements of the problem but does not distort them.

The brief life of the Republic of the Congo has been stormy from birth. An initial rivalry for leadership between Patrice Lumumba and Joseph Kasavubu was composed for a time by a division of offices, Lumumba becoming prime minister and Kasavubu chief of state. In the early weeks, however, Katanga, the richest province of the republic, rejected the authority of the central government and struck out on an independent course under Moise Tshombe. In the smaller neighboring state of Kasai, Albert Kalonji also pursued a separatist policy.

Lumumba, an impassioned centralist, insisted upon a unitary state. For a time at least, Kasavubu appears to have leaned toward a federal organization of the republic, but he lapsed into inactivity, leaving the field to Lumumba. Lumumba threatened Katanga and railed at Tshombe. Tshombe remained unimpressed, secure in the economic resources of Katanga. His regime was nourished by revenues from the Société Haute Minière du Congo, the powerful Belgian copper-mining enterprise of the province, and he persevered in his claim to autonomy. The dissensions among Katanga, Kasai, and the central regime at Leopoldville were the most conspicuous disturbances in a general disorder.

Independence had come suddenly to the Congo, and it found the population excited by the prospect but unprepared to receive it. Some seven weeks after the inception of the new regime, the Belgian Minister of African Affairs acknowledged that Belgium had "delayed in forming a Congolese official class. As a result, he said, the process of putting the Congolese in charge of running their country could not have been carried out without a shock." [1] The Minister exhibited a gift for understatement. Many of the Congolese, a people of fourteen million thinly distributed through a vast area, territorially the largest of the new African states, were neither able nor disposed to distinguish between freedom and unfettered irresponsibility. They cut loose. Their feelings erupted in personal vendettas, tribal feuds, and attacks upon individual Belgians as representatives of the former colonial rule. The Congolese *Force Publique,* a constabulary organized by the Belgian army, became infected by the turmoil and mutinied. Alarmed by the peril to its nationals, Belgium maintained its garrisons and even returned some troops that had been withdrawn.

Belgium's retention of military forces in the Congo infuriated Lumumba, who declined to credit the stated Belgian motives. He associated the act with the support given Tshombe by Belgians in Katanga, as phases of a maneuver by Belgium to retain the control that had been ostensibly relinquished. Whether through personal preference or lack of any real choice, Tshombe had accepted the continued presence of the Belgians in Katanga, not

[1] *The New York Times,* August 18, 1960, p. 3.

47

only in copper mining and general industry but also in the provincial administration itself. Lumumba denounced Tshombe as a stooge of the Belgians, bracketing Katanga and Belgium as prime enemies of Congolese independence. Powerless to push the Belgians out, unable to subdue Katanga, and worried by the insubordination of the Congolese *Force Publique*, the Prime Minister turned to the United Nations for help.

The appeal touched off an acrid dispute within the United Nations. The Soviet Union, assuming a role as champion of the Congolese struggle for liberation, echoed Lumumba's condemnation of Belgium and Tshombe, demanding that the United Nations take steps to compel the withdrawal of the one and liquidate the secession of the other. It even threatened to take measures of its own to force "hands off the Congo." The United States and other NATO powers did not conceal their distrust of the Soviet Union's intentions. All recognized a danger that the vacuum of effective government within the Congo might suck in the great powers. The Secretary General, Dag Hammarskjöld, who bore the main burden of the United Nations' endeavor to pacify the Congo until he lost his life in the attempt, gave voice to the general fear. "The problem facing the Congo," he reported to the Security Council on August 8, 1960, "is one of peace or war—and not only in the Congo." The United Nations, he warned, must respond to Lumumba's appeal and exclude "conflicts extraneous to the African world" from the Republic of the Congo.

In the tense summer of 1960, the United Nations

Operation in the Congo was established, called ONUC, from its French initials. ONUC furnished a military force recruited from states other than the great powers, notably in the first instance Ethiopia, Ghana, Morocco, Tunisia, Guinea, Mali, Sweden, and Ireland. In time, the force grew to over 19,000 men from thirteen nations. ONUC also comprised a civilian component. Its military activities caught the public eye throughout the world, but its civilian effort is even more revealing of the gap between the acquisition of political power and the conduct of government in the Republic of the Congo.

From the outset, ONUC collided with Lumumba. The Prime Minister and the Secretary General differed radically in their conception of ONUC's function. Lumumba demanded that ONUC expel the Belgians, break Katanga's resistance, and subdue the mutinous *Force Publique*. In his view, ONUC had no other mission; except as it discharged this mission, it had no reason to exist. The Prime Minister's interpretation was endorsed by a number of the other new African states, and won quick support from the Soviet Union. The Secretary General pointed out that the function of ONUC, as an instrument of the United Nations, must remain consistent with the United Nations Charter. Under the Charter, it was the duty of the United Nations to check threats to international peace, breaches of the peace, and international acts of aggression, but it must not mix in matters essentially within the domestic jurisdiction of any state.

Since the continued deployment of Belgian troops in the Congo raised an international hazard, the United

Nations and ONUC as its instrument had to force Belgium's withdrawal. Here the Secretary General had no difficulty in finding common ground with Lumumba. The maintenance of internal order was quite another matter. It was a touchy point, and a fine line had to be drawn. Essentially, internal disorder involved a domestic responsibility. When such disorder widened and deepened into a total breakdown that invited intervention from outside, its character changed. It ceased to be solely domestic and became a threat to international peace. Unavoidably, the responsibility of the United Nations became involved, and ONUC could not stand aloof. But the United Nations could not and would not choose between rival assertions of internal political authority.

The Security Council, in its resolution of August 9, 1960, supported Hammarskjöld's view. The resolution called upon Belgium to withdraw its troops from Katanga without delay, but affirmed that ONUC "will not be a party to or in any way intervene in or be used to influence the outcome of any internal conflict, constitutional or otherwise." Neither Hammarskjöld's patient explanations nor ONUC's energetic services reduced the Prime Minister's intransigence. The rift widened and became uglier. Events in time removed Lumumba, but thereafter took a twist that brought ONUC's actions in Katanga, though not its motivation, into line with Lumumba's desire.

In September, 1960, the Chief of State, Joseph Kasavubu, quiescent through the summer, suddenly came to life. He charged Lumumba with fomenting internal discord, abridging the fundamental liberties of citizens, and diverting the Republic of the Congo from its proper course into a civil war. In Kasavubu's view, Lumumba had violated his trust and forfeited his right to office. The Chief of State dismissed the Prime Minister and his government and called upon the President of the Congolese Senate, Joseph Ileo, to form a new government. In an effort to forestall an explosive reaction, Kasavubu formally requested ONUC to assure peace and order. Lumumba responded with characteristic fervor. In repeated broadcasts, he proclaimed that Kasavubu had ceased to be Chief of State. He made no effort to counter Kasavubu's appeal to ONUC, but called instead upon the people of the Congo, the workers, and the army to rise and rally to his banner. The Council of Ministers supported Lumumba, accusing the Chief of State of high treason. The Congolese Parliament moved into the fray, and its Chamber of Representatives purported to cancel the mutual dismissals of the Prime Minister and the Chief of State. In an effort to contain the conflict, ONUC closed the airports and the radio station of the capital. Despite its pacific purpose, the action embroiled ONUC in the constitutional dispute. Lumumba accused the United Nations of flagrant interference in the constitutional affairs of the Congo. Kasavubu and Lumumba each demanded that ONUC recognize his paramount authority and terminate relations with the other.

The comic tragedy hurried on. Joseph Mobutu, the Chief of Staff of the Congolese army, broadcast an announcement that the army could no longer tolerate the mutual frustration of the two alleged governments and was taking power. He described the take-over as a peaceful revolution and fixed its duration, setting a terminal date of December 31, 1960. Lumumba fled to a refuge in the officer's mess of the Ghana contingent of ONUC's military force in Leopoldville. Like Lumumba, Kasavubu, and Ileo as Kasavubu's nominee, Mobutu called for exclusive support from ONUC. In a report to the Secretary General, the Special Representative of the Secretary General in the Congo described ONUC's plight with meticulous restraint:

> It is obvious that in so complex and variable a situation, the imperative of non-intervention requires continuous analysis and careful weighing by ONUC in the context of rapidly unfolding events. During the protracted political crises, while ONUC has maintained an attitude of strict detachment, it has not been one of indifference to the point of denying the possibility of the exercise of the function of good offices, should it be sought by all concerned.[2]

From time to time, Lumumba threatened to summon help for his cause from other sources, leaving no doubt that he had the Soviet Union chiefly in mind. In the September turmoil, Lumumba may have turned to the representatives of Communist governments in the Congo, or they may have approached him. Mobutu, at any rate, evidently thought so. On September 16, under his asserted authority as Chief of Staff of the army and chief of the government, he ordered the diplomatic

[2] *United Nations Review,* November 1960, p. 19.

missions of the Soviet Union and Czechoslovakia out of the Congo, together with all their technicians. Mobutu's suspicions of intrigue subsequently extended to President Nkrumah of Ghana, who appears to have volunteered advice to Lumumba in letters addressed to the latter as "Dear Patrice." In November, Mobutu expelled Nkrumah's personal representative from the Congo. At this point, the endemic disease of factionalism seems to have infected a part of ONUC itself. Troops from ONUC's Tunisian contingent tried to block the execution of Mobutu's order of expulsion, and clashed with Congolese troops.

Through Antoine Gizenga, a close associate, Lumumba kept in touch with Congolese followers who shared not only his views concerning the Congo but his readiness to seek Communist support. The Lumumba-Gizenga faction gathered in Stanleyville, the capital of Oriental Province of the republic. At the end of November, Lumumba suddenly disappeared from sight. He reappeared in early December as a prisoner of Mobutu. The general charged that Lumumba had been intercepted while on his way to Stanleyville to lead an insurrection by his following. The regime had therefore arrested Lumumba in self-defense. He was held in custody for a month. In January, 1961, Kasavubu, who had reasserted his authority with Mobutu's support, turned Lumumba over to Moise Tshombe, the President of Katanga. The transfer has never been publicly explained. Among the many criss-crossing lines of rivalry in the Congo, none was more bitter than the enmity between Lumumba and Tshombe, and the consequences could have been foreseen. A month after becoming Tshombe's captive, Lumumba reached the end of his trail. He was shot and killed, allegedly by Katangese villagers while he was attempting to escape. A UN investigating committee subsequently concluded that he had probably been murdered at Tshombe's orders.

Gizenga promptly proclaimed himself Lumumba's heir. He purported to establish a government based upon Stanleyville, claiming it to be the only lawful government of the republic. The old rivalry between Kasavubu and Lumumba thus received a geographical expression. Since Tshombe maintained his position in Katanga, the Congo was torn by a three-way dispute over political authority, supplemented by such minor cleavages as that of Kalonji in the province of Kasai and random bursts of disorder.

In 1962, the central regime managed to extract one thorn from its flesh by arresting and incarcerating Gizenga, but Tshombe persevered. At the United Nations, opinion gradually crystallized into a conviction that the Katangese secession had become a threat to international peace. When a series of new attempts to end the secession in negotiations between Tshombe and the Prime Minister at Leopoldville proved abortive, ONUC moved into Katanga with decisive military force. Tshombe's resistance was finally broken, and early in 1963 Katanga submitted to absorption by the regime.

The incorporation of Katanga and Tshombe's disappearance to more comfortable surroundings in Paris did not suffice to restore tranquillity. Tribal and regional dissension persisted, and Lumumba's ghost walked.

54

Some of the rebellious elements, proclaiming their fidelity to the memory of Lumumba, clustered together in a self-styled "government in exile" in Brazzaville, the capital of the neighboring Congo Republic which had been established in a province of former French Equatorial Africa. An earlier cycle of intrigue, suspicion, and reaction that had culminated in Mobutu's ejection of the Soviet Union's ambassador in September, 1960, recurred in 1963. In the interval, the USSR had restored its diplomatic representation. In November, 1963, Adoula, who had succeeded Ileo as Prime Minister of the Republic of the Congo, accused the Soviet Union of conspiring with the "government in exile" and expelled the ambassador and his entire staff. But Adoula found no rest for the weary and in 1964, in effect acknowledging the situation to be beyond him, he relinquished his office.

The choice of his successor introduced a new note of irony into the turbulent sequence of events. Moise Tshombe was recalled from his refuge in Paris to assume the chief political responsibility in Leopoldville. As Prime Minister, he sought to vindicate the national supremacy of the regime against which he had so relentlessly fought. Tshombe and his colleagues had to muster troops of their own to a degree unknown by a Congolese regime through all but the first six or seven weeks of the republic's existence, for on June 30, 1964, the United Nations Force, the military component of ONUC, left the Congo.

Its departure did not signal a judgment that the internal disputes in the Congo were sufficiently under control to make its presence unnecessary. Financial embarrassment had entered into the decision. The Soviet Union, France, and others had refused to pay their share of the assessments required to meet the growing costs of the United Nations Force. A controversy had ensued that could not be resolved in time to permit a decision based solely on an appraisal of the need.

The Secretary General, however, saw some virtue in the necessity. He believed that "apart from the financial difficulty . . . a further extension of the stay of the Force in the Congo would provide no solution to the remaining problems. . . . The United Nations cannot permanently protect the Congo, or any other country, from the internal tensions and disturbances created by its own organic growth toward unity and nationhood. This is an undertaking which henceforth must be carried out only by the Government and the people of the Congo." There had to be a "retraining and reorganization of the National Army, including the training of a substantial officer corps" and "reconciliation amongst the contending political leaders and factions." [3]

We may assume that Tshombe perceived the need more readily than the means to satisfy it. An insurgent faction proclaimed a "People's Republic of the Congo" with its headquarters at Stanleyville, the seat of Gizenga's earlier pretension to lawful authority and the original rallying point of Lumumba's followers. One Christophe Gbenye, who appears to have been the Minister of the Interior in Lumumba's sometime cabinet, styled himself the President of the "People's Republic." He seems to

[3] 1 UN Monthly Chronicle, July 1964, p. 32.

have set himself to lay about in all directions. In radio broadcasts, he not only excoriated Tshombe and the central regime, but declared the People's Republic "at war with the United States" and accused the United Nations of importing "murderous devices under the name of food and medicine" in order to "massacre the Congolese people." [4] In Tshombe's view, Gbenye's fine frenzy was abetted if not stimulated by the Communist People's Republic of China, maneuvering through its legations in the Congo Republic (Brazzaville) and the tiny state of Burundi that bordered the Republic of the Congo in the east. In September, 1964, Tshombe sought assistance from the other African states deliberating under the auspices of the Organization of African Unity. His African colleagues offered advice and established a nine-member Congo Reconciliation Commission, but showed no sign of providing the troops or materials he requested. Whether on his own or under external prodding, Tshombe took help where he could find it, employing white mercenary troops. The step endeared him to no one, and roused Ben Bella in Algeria and Nasser in the United Arab Republic to peaks of outraged virtue. They put teeth into their hostility by infiltrating aid to the insurgents. The Foreign Minister of Senegal protested that "There is a kind of internal imperialism in Africa. Some of the states here seem even to want to impose their own regimes on all of Africa." [5]

By March of 1965, the Organization of African Unity

[4] *The New York Times*, Sept. 19, 1964, p. 5.
[5] *The New York Times*, March 8, 1965, p. 7.

had divided into mutually vituperative camps. One denounced Tshombe as a puppet of Belgium and the United States. Another supported him without enthusiasm on the principle of nonintervention, insisting that the principle applied against intrusions by Communist China, the United Arab Republic, and Algeria no less than by European or North American states. A third group abstained from any position on the Congo's internal affairs. In April, Tshombe reinforced his status by holding and winning an election from which he emerged as a "constitutional Prime Minister," Kasavubu being re-elected President. Fortune smiled in a measure on Tshombe's arms, as the regime's forces drove the insurgents from their "capital" at Stanleyville and shattered them into three dispersed fragments and random guerrilla splinters. In the summer of 1965, the Congo "face[d] at least three years of mopping up among roaming bands of outlaws."[6]

Through the smoke of the protracted civil conflict, facts can be discerned in the Congo experience that have prime importance for our present inquiry. While the rival claimants each wielded political power of a sort within their respective geographical spheres, none succeeded in making the transition from the taking of power to the conduct of government. Lumumba, Kasavubu, Ileo, and Mobutu could take power in Leopoldville, Tshombe in Katanga, and Gizenga and Gbenye for a time in Stanleyville. Yet none ever really governed. The causes must be brought to light and examined. The failure is generally attributed to the unpreparedness of the Congolese for

[6] Ibid., June 13, 1965, p. 20.

self-government. The explanation can be accepted, but it must be probed for a full appreciation of its meaning.

In one sense, the preparation of a dependent people for self-government involves a carefully arranged and timed transfer of management of the administrative machinery and the central public services of the state. The men who are to receive the transfer of powers must first be identified. The identification entails an accord between the retiring regime and the dependent people. They must agree as to who will do what. Such an agreement can only be reached if there are spokesmen through whom the dependent people can express their assent. The authority of the spokesmen to represent the people must be established through procedures appropriate to their habits and outlook. Without such a prior arrangement, the withdrawal of the old regime is bound to precipitate a scramble for place among ambitious and opportunistic men, a breakdown in services, and general bewilderment among the populace. The more abrupt the withdrawal, the greater will be the confusion. The Belgian government failed in this sense to prepare the Congolese for their independence.

There is also another and deeper level of meaning to the preparation of a dependent people for self-government. However earnest the desire and careful the arrangement and timing, the management of public services and administrative machinery cannot be transferred unless men are available who can take over the managerial functions. In the Republic of the Congo, such men could not be found. With negligible exceptions, they simply did not exist. When ONUC entered the Congo, it was compelled to substitute for them and improvise a civilian administration. In a little more than a month, it assembled the largest civilian operating group ever organized anywhere under UN auspices. The size and extent of the UN's civilian operation in the Congo can perhaps best be indicated by listing some of the services that would not have been provided at all without it. The Special Representative of the Secretary General in the Congo incorporated such a list in his first Progress Report on September 21, 1960:

. . . There was an immediate and country-wide breakdown in the regular commercial arrangements for distributing food, to the point where people in some parts of the Congo must now rely for their main sustenance on food supplies distributed from Leopoldville by the United Nations. There was, at the same time, the threat of a major breakdown in the maintenance of water supply and sanitation facilities. Without the services of World Health Organization personnel, who arrived within two days of the plea for help, these facilities might have failed. . . .

. . . there was virtually no trained staff to supervise the operation of telephone, telegraph, telex and radio transmission installations, and these facilities are in operation today only because of the presence of a large United Nations and International Telecommunication Union team. Likewise, air traffic control services were deteriorating with the departure of technicians from a very large number of airports. Today, adequate servicing of flights can only be assured at the three airports where United Nations advisers, controllers and radio technicians are based. If there were not any meteorologists assigned by the United Nations to the country (there are five), there would be absolutely no meteorological protection for planes. . . .

At the beginning of the crisis, in July, almost all surface transportation had become paralyzed for lack of security and supervisory arrangements. This traffic has now been put into motion again, but at a lower level of efficiency and on an uncertain basis. The vital port of Matadi, for example, is running now because ONUC opened it to traffic and assured the continuation of dredging and pilot operations. The United Nations has taken measures to ensure the passage of rail freight through Kasai Province into Katanga, and from Matadi to Leopoldville.

In the all-important sector of finance and trade, ONUC stepped in to sound the alarm and suggest control measures at a time when there was a possibility of foreign exchange being completely exhausted. The flight of capital from the country, which had begun several years previously, is being brought under control by hastily improvised economic and financial measures. In the area of labor administration, the entire social security system has been, and to an extent still is, threatened by collapse. For the time being, the system of labor inspection has been suspended. For this service, and for the completely depleted statistical offices of the Government, substantial United Nations assistance has been requested. The collapse of the judiciary and court system has given rise to very serious problems affecting the administration of justice; a legal consultant has recently arrived and is faced with the very difficult task of helping to set up judicial machinery in the absence of trained Congolese judges and magistrates.

. . . . .

. . . An agreement for the liquidation of the old Central Bank of the Congo and Ruanda-Urundi was entered into between Congolese and Belgian officials a month ago under United Nations auspices. Moreover, United Nations advisers assisted in the preparation of proposals for the creation of an interim organization to operate after the liquidation and before the establishment of a new Central Bank. As a result of the recent political crisis, no action has been taken, and the Government is still not in a position to create money and credit.[7]

The United Nations' purpose in the Congo remains the elimination of threats to international peace. The purpose must be realized in the circumstances as they exist. In the actual circumstances as appraised by the UN through bitter trial and error, the purpose can best be achieved through the establishment of a stable and independent regime in the Congo in accordance with the wishes of the inhabitants. To bring such a regime into being has become the operating objective of the UN's

[7] *United Nations Review*, November 1960, pp. 20–21.

continuing civilian assistance. By its very nature, the objective requires the withdrawal of ONUC in due time. The Secretary General never lost sight of this ultimate requirement. Mindful of his experience with the military component, he was painfully aware that financial stringency, political pressures or unforeseen events might compel such a withdrawal from the civilian sector long before it was "due."

Foreseeing the eventual withdrawal of its civilian component, ONUC has striven to make the Congolese ready. Through all the turmoil, it has supplemented its emergency activities by systematic efforts to prepare for the longer term. It has designed "a structural basis for the civil service" and has engaged in the "training of Congolese professionals and technicians, in terms of accelerated in-service courses being prepared in the Congo, as well as scholarship programs abroad of short and long duration." [8] Here is an effort described in terms reminiscent of an annual report by a dean of a school of public administration that yet goes to the heart of a major contemporary human and political process. ONUC is striving to supply a basic and indispensable resource, men qualified to operate the machinery of a modern state. "The United Nations has learned very much from its experience in the Congo thus far; in the circumstances, much of that experience could only be unhappy. Fundamentally, what it has learned there is that the Congolese, in education, training and experience, and even in their understanding of the concept of nation-

[8] Ibid., January 1961, p. 26.

hood, were unprepared to assume the responsibilities of independence. . . ." [9] ONUC is racing against time, and hampered in the race by the tangle of Congolese cross-purposes. In its objectives, nature, and handicaps, the race has a representative significance. It is a particular manifestation of a problem generally encountered in the newly emerging and developing societies.

Despite the marvels of modern science and technology, and indeed to some extent because of them, it takes time —decades—to produce qualified men and women. Roughly twenty years of growth and training are required to bring a person from his birth to a level of education represented by the ordinary first university degree, and additional years are necessary to turn him into a physicist, biochemist, physician, economist, engineer, agronomist, lawyer, accountant, or civil servant. Educators in all lands are seeking to accelerate the process, but their efforts are largely frustrated by the growing accumulation of knowledge and technique to be imparted. Whatever success may be achieved in accelerating the course of education and training, it is improbable that the time required to produce a qualified and trained human being can be significantly reduced below two decades, even when the basic human material is good.

Such men and women are the indispensable means for modernizing a society. Science, technology, and modern industrial organization can be incorporated into a society

[9] From the Secretary General's Report to the Security Council, June 30, 1964, in *1 UN Monthly Chronicle* (July 1964), p. 32.

64

only by instilling into a sufficient number of its people knowledge of the accumulated learning, mastery of the techniques, and an understanding of the outlook and methods by which science renews and extends itself. There is no other way. It cannot be done by importing goods. It cannot be done by purchasing—or obtaining gifts of—facilities or equipment. It cannot be done through the construction of factories, airports, or school buildings by foreign architects, engineers, and artisans temporarily employed or borrowed for the purpose. It cannot be done by proclamations or parades, mass terror, or mass exhilaration. These are facts that cannot be escaped. But for reasons previously explained, the facts are seldom appreciated in all their implications.

We have already observed the effect which the prestige of modern science, technology, and industrial organization has had upon the minds of men, even in the advanced industrial states and particularly in the emerging societies. Their expectations are expanded; they are unable or unwilling to recognize the unavoidable limitations; they are in a hurry to enjoy the benefits; and they press their political leaders for prompt and conspicuous achievements. It is hard for them to understand and accept the scale and duration of the effort required to produce the qualified men and women without whom the job cannot be done. In their impatience and ignorance, they may insist upon conduct that impedes the effort or they may resist behavior required to make it effective. They may thus unwittingly frustrate the achievement of the very goals they seek.

Through time and experience, they can learn to adjust their expectations and to support the needed programs of education and training for the length of time required. Technical assistance from outside can help. Above all, wise and enlightened leadership of their own can enlist their sympathy and understanding and induce them to do what must be done. As in the Republic of the Congo, however, time may be hard to get and experience may hurt. Those who can give technical assistance may find it difficult to give. Forceful and constructive leadership from within may be rare. When such leadership does arise, it may have trouble competing with politicians of another sort who promise quick and easy results.

In the newly emerging states, the discrepancies between the qualities needed to win political power and those needed to govern are manifested with a peculiar poignancy.

CHAPTER V

THE BRITISH
ACCOMMODATION

However adequately organized the 'political' side of
government, however wise our political philosophy and
high leadership and command, these would be of no
effect without a body of officials expert in applying
the accumulated supply of power and the general wisdom
to particular cases, and permanently and specially employed to do so.

H. Finer, *The British Civil Service*

At its head stood . . . a yet more formidable figure,
the Permanent Under-Secretary himself, . . . a man
remarkable even among civil servants for adroitness
in baffling inconvenient inquiries, resource in raising
false issues, and, in short, a consummate command of
all the arts of officially sticking in the mud.

Lytton Strachey, "Florence Nightingale"

In American popular opinion during the past hundred
years the government of England has been widely es-
teemed for its accommodation between the struggle for
political power and the conduct of government. If American popular appreciation outruns the popular understanding of what in fact has happened in British politics
and government, it nevertheless has support in better
informed and more critical appraisals. Both general and

trained opinion have identified the career services as a notable factor in the British accomplishment.

The Civil Service and the Foreign Service of Britain in the form that has won renown are comparatively recent in origin. They do not antedate the middle of the nineteenth century. Many Englishmen indeed enjoyed careers as civil officers of the Crown in prior centuries, in the sense of long and stable tenure of posts compensated out of the national treasury, but they were scarcely public servants of the type evoked in contemporary minds by a reference to the British career services.

In the seventeenth and eighteenth centuries and well into the nineteenth, effortless and comfortable posts in the government were granted and accepted without embarrassment as perquisites of the aristocracy. Sinecures and pensions served not only as the coin of political patronage but as genteel alms for indigent noblemen. Powerful families tended to regard them with proprietary eyes:

In 1809, the annual net value of the principal sinecures was £356,555 and these were held, almost without exception, by members of the aristocracy. They ranged from positions like Keeper of the Privy Seal for Scotland to that of Sweeper of the Mall in the Park, the latter place being, for a time, the proud possession of a baroness.

The pension roll, too, was crowded with the representatives and dependents of the great families. At one period there were six members of the family of Lord

Bathurst on the list, six or eight Greys, five Beresfords, a numerous host associated with the Wellesley family, Mulgraves, Manchesters, Morningtons. Indeed, the Civil List was a roster of the politically active aristocracy, together with their illegitimate children, cast-off employees, mistresses, and poor relations.[1]

John Bright in the nineteenth century vented his contempt for the practice in a famous phrase, when he called the Foreign Office "the outdoor relief department of the aristocracy," but in the eighteenth century, Edmund Burke looked upon the arrangements as a fitting part of the proper order of things. Few of his contemporaries matched Burke in understanding the "disorders" and "infirmities" of the British government of the time, and none advocated reform with equal eloquence and insight. In his famous speech on the "Economical Reformation of the Civil and other Establishments," Burke pressed the House of Commons "to consider the wisdom of a timely reform," pointing out that "neither the present, nor any other first lord of the Treasury, has ever been able to take a survey, or to make even a tolerable guess, of the expenses of government for any one year." He called for the abolition of all offices "which furnish more matter of expense . . . or more means and instruments of corrupt influence than advantage to justice or political administration" or "which bring more charge than proportional advantage to the state." Yet he wanted to retain many offices which he acknowledged "to be no better

[1] J. Donald Kingsley: *Representative Bureaucracy* (Yellow Springs, Ohio: The Antioch Press; 1944), pp. 27–28.

than pensions," on the ground that there must be means "of furnishing a permanent reward to public service, of making that reward the origin of families, and the foundation of wealth as well as of honours." He deplored "the unseemly spectacle" and the "disgrace" that it would be "to see the hopeful son of a meritorious minister begging his bread at the door of that treasury from whence his father dispensed the economy of an empire. . . ." He was happy to find "the exchequer list . . . filled with the descendants of the Walpoles, of the Pelhams, and the Townshends—names to whom this country owes its liberties. . . . May such fountains never be dried up."

Burke's attitude typified the pervasive acceptance of the practice, shared even by William Cobbett, the Radical champion of the poor working class of rural England, himself the son of a small farmer and grandson of a day laborer. Cobbett's approval survived even a poignant personal experience. In 1791, while serving as a sergeant-major in the British army, he was shocked to discover widespread fraud and embezzlement in his regiment. Collecting much evidence, he undertook to punish the culprits, even to the point of demanding a court-martial of the participating officers. He learned to his sorrow that he was tilting at windmills, and was forced to take refuge in flight, first to France and then to the United States. Nevertheless, when back in England years later, he wrote in the *Political Register* on March 1, 1806, that government posts "now serve, or ought to serve, the purpose of rewarding public services . . . and

70

. . . of upholding and cherishing those amongst the ancient nobility and gentry, who otherwise might fall into a state that would inevitably bring disgrace upon rank. . . ." [2]

It is hard to trace the line between patronage in the usual political sense and the charitable bestowal of offices in eighteenth-century England, or the line between patronage and the assertion of a kind of proprietary claim to particular offices. One blended into the other, and the blend reflected the structure of eighteenth-century English politics. Political power was divided between the Crown and Parliament, that of the former diminishing and that of the latter growing in a steady transfer of sovereignty from the king to the House of Commons following the revolution of 1688–89. In time, the triumph of Parliament would become the triumph of popular government, but in the reign of William and Mary and the Hanoverian kings, it only raised a group of aristocratic families to control in the state. Edmund Burke may have persuaded himself that the "value, spirit, and essence of a House of Commons consists in its being the express image of the feelings of the nation," but the facts appear to have been described more accurately by a critic's outburst that "This House is not a representative of the people of Great Britain. It is the representative of nominal boroughs, of ruined and exterminated towns, of noble families, of wealthy individuals. . . ." [3]

[2] Cobbett's *Political Register*, IX, 315 (1806).
[3] Quoted in Green: *History of the English People*, University Edition (New York: Sully and Kleinteich), VI, 19.

Two hundred years earlier, Henry VIII had packed Parliament to bring it to heel. His Tudor successors continued the practice. They created new boroughs and vested the right to send members to Parliament in boroughs until then without representation, expanding the House of Commons by more than a hundred members. The convenient artifice came to be appreciated by the great landowners, who in time through tenacious opportunism gradually took control of it. While cities like Birmingham and Manchester went without representation in Parliament, members were returned by boroughs of trivial size or significance, in some cases boroughs which had actually ceased to exist. The contrived seats became a form of property bought and sold by noble families on the open market, somewhat as seats on stock and commodity exchanges are today. The prices varied. At one point, a borough sold for £4,000. The Duke of Newcastle, the very model of an eighteenth-century English minister, stood out in the parliamentary traffic, controlling a third of the boroughs that sent members to the House. It was not the Whigs or Tories as political parties but their members as individual landowners who controlled the boroughs and claimed the various sectors of patronage.

Parliament as an institution represented its members and the landowners who sent them to Westminster. Little attempt was made to cover the facts under virtuous protestations that Parliament represented the people of England. The eighteenth-century Parliament not only acknowledged its character but insisted upon it. Its

72

members rejected any suggestion that they represented the people or were obligated to do so. They ignored public opinion with open contempt. Not until the rise of William Pitt in the middle of the century did general public opinion find a voice in Parliament, and the opinion that supported Pitt was general and public only in a comparative sense. The Great Commoner was the champion of the emerging urban middle class. His pride in the "people who have sent me here" was warranted in contrast with the proprietary position of the Walpoles, Pelhams, Newcastles, and Grenvilles, but his "people" were mainly the wealthier merchants. Even Pitt found his way into Parliament through a pocket borough that had been acquired by his father, presumably with funds inherited from Pitt's wealthy grandfather, a former governor of Madras. Neither Pitt's extraordinary talent, his popularity among the commercial middle class, nor the genuine recognition in Parliament of his brilliance and energy sufficed to make him effective. He had to come to terms with the men who had taken Parliament as their preserve, and "borrowed the Duke of Newcastle's majority to carry on the public business."

The parties of the period were not parties of the kind familiar to Englishmen today. The Whigs who, with brief lapses, dominated Parliament for three quarters of a century following the Revolution of 1688–89, were a group of noblemen and their kin and retainers, joined together originally in a political alliance against the Stuart kings culminating in the removal of James II and the exclusion of the Catholic members of his line from the succession to the throne. They were not without a bond of common aims and ideas in the early decades after the Glorious Revolution. They were the protagonists in the installation of William and Mary upon the throne vacated by James II, the elevation of Anne as Queen when William and Mary died without issue, and the inauguration of the Hanoverian line of kings through the accession of George I when Anne died without heirs. But after definitive limits were set to the royal power, parliamentary control was established over the national purse, and England was launched upon the course that led in time to the unchallenged supremacy of Parliament, the will to maintain the power of Parliament against possible encroachment by the Crown on one side and a rising commercial middle class on the other became virtually the only important continuing element of common purpose in the Whig Party.

For some decades after the Revolution of 1688–89, the Tory gentry sulked in their tents. When at long last they ended their flirtation with the Stuart pretenders, transferred to the new line of kings their old attachment to the Crown and the Church, and re-entered the arena of parliamentary politics in force, they differed little from the Whigs in looseness of party organization and diffusion of purpose.

George III wrestled with Parliament toward the close of the eighteenth century in a drive to recapture effective sovereignty for the Crown, and employed the arts and crafts of bribery and political jobbery. Under the competitive stimulus of royal attack and parliamentary response, the scale and crudity of patronage reached a new high.

74

But it did not involve the recurrent wholesale changes of personnel that featured the "spoils system" in the history of American politics. Security of tenure there was, after a fashion, with the consequent advantages of continuity, if continuity may be thought to have advantages when the character of the public service is so largely determined by political corruption. The Whig and Tory families showed a fine mutual understanding and forbearance toward their respective political retainers and impecunious relatives, who were not often stricken from the rolls of the "outdoor relief department of the aristocracy." There was no need to do so if the public pay rolls could be expanded, and expanded they were from Cabinet to Cabinet.

Patronage gradually changed in character in the early decades of the nineteenth century but did not significantly diminish. As the parties evolved toward a condition more nearly like that of parties today, the personal and proprietary use of patronage became a sore point. Party leaders sought to convert the practice into an instrument of party organization and power. By the 1820's, the Whigs had made enough headway toward concentrating control over patronage in party hands for party purposes to gratify Lord John Russell, but much of the proprietary attitude of powerful families toward political jobs and sinecures hung on. A letter from Disraeli illuminated the situation in the Conservative Party, the lineal descendant of the Tory Party, as late as 1858:

> I cannot but feel that there is a great error on the part of some of my colleagues on the subject of

patronage. They are too apt to deem the preferment at their disposal to be merely a personal privilege. In my opinion, it partakes of a corporate character. . . .

The spirit of the party in the country depends greatly on the distribution of patronage: none can be more aware of this than Lord Derby and myself. . . .

The interests of the party can never require an improper appointment: an improper appointment is a job, and nothing injures a party more than a job. But, at the same time, there is nothing more ruinous to political connection than the fear of justly rewarding your friends, and the promotion of ordinary men of opposite opinions in preference to qualified adherents. It is not becoming in any Minister to decry party who has risen by party. We should always remember that if we were not partisans, we should not be Ministers. . . .[4]

As the parties centralized control over patronage for party purposes, they tightened their organization and their leadership gained in internal control. Although the changes in the practice of patronage, the growth in party cohesiveness, and the gain in power of the party leadership coincided, it is not easy to sort out the patterns of cause and effect among them. The causal relationships appear to have been reciprocal, each change stimulating and stimulated by the others.

[4] Monypenny and Buckle: *The Life of Benjamin Disraeli* (London, 1929), I, 1657–8.

Prior to the accession of William and Mary to the throne, ministers had been the servants of the King in Parliament. The several ministers were mutually independent, each selected by the King and responsible to him alone. But with the transfer of power from the Crown to Parliament in the Revolution of 1688–89 that elevated William and Mary to the throne, ministers of the old style became useless to the King. William at first picked his ministers in the old way but became mired in frustration. He could extricate himself only by acknowledging the new power of the Parliament in his choice of ministers and selecting men from the dominant party in the House of Commons whom the House regarded as its own. Still nominally the servants of the King, they became actually the servants of the House which they led. They worked together as a group and served a dual function as a committee of advisers to the King and a kind of executive committee to the House of Commons.

The transformation in the nature of ministers and the relationships among them developed slowly under William and Mary and Queen Anne, but accelerated with the accession of George I in 1714. Speaking only German, George I found attendance at the meetings of his ministers unbearably tedious, and absented himself. Meeting alone solidified the group character of the Cabinet. In the absence of the King from Cabinet meetings, a minister had to preside. By a natural evolution, particular ministers came to preside with regularity, and the customary chairman came to be recognized as the first minister. As the Cabinet and the first minister slowly acquired the

77

attributes familiar today, their function as a committee of advisers to the King was gradually absorbed into their function as an executive committee of the House of Commons, and their function as the executive committee of the House ripened into the executive leadership of the government of England. Some historians identify Sir Robert Walpole, who presided in the Cabinet from 1721 to 1742, as the first "true" Prime Minister. Others assign that distinction to Sir Robert Peel, who first became Prime Minister for a brief period in 1835 and again for a more extended period in 1841. In so doing, they emphasize the political implications of the Reform Act of 1832.

The Act diminished the political power of the great landowning families by striking at one of its sources. It denied any further representation in the House to fifty-six "pocket" and "rotten" boroughs that had been returning one hundred and eleven members to Parliament, and reduced the representation of thirty-two small boroughs from two to one member each. One hundred and forty-three seats tightly controlled under the old dispensation thus became available for redistribution among the towns and counties on a more nearly representative basis. Twenty-two large English towns received two seats, twenty-one smaller English towns each a single seat, thirteen seats were allotted to Scotland and Ireland, and the remainder were distributed in the counties. At the same time, the Act extended the right to vote to persons meeting specified property and taxpaying qualifications who previously had not enjoyed the franchise. While the reform fell far short of universal or even general suffrage, it enfranchised a segment of the middle class that, while not large in absolute terms, was large enough to give a new cast to electoral politics. The extension of the suffrage and the reapportionment of seats away from the rotten and pocket boroughs and the families that had controlled them gave a new meaning to public opinion and parliamentary representation.

As elections came to turn more and more upon public approval, the parties based their appeals to the electorate increasingly upon policies and personalities. Electoral success came to involve a growing measure of commitment to particular policies and political leaders. There was a corresponding gain in the importance of policies and party leadership as the bonds that held each party together and shaped its character. The enhanced cohesiveness of the parties and strength of the party leadership helped to promote corporate party control over patronage, and party solidarity and party leadership were in turn reinforced by the new grip on patronage. The advances in party organization and responsiveness to public opinion and in the political power of the middle class ran parallel and contributed to a transformation in British public administration.

The Reform Act of 1832 was neither the first nor the last step in the expansion of democracy in nineteenth-century England. The ideas of the American Revolution and the French Revolution that spread popular participation in government and a creed of human rights in continental Europe and North America had their counterparts and precursors in England. The distinction drawn by Burke in 1790 in his *Reflections on the Revolution in France* between the true liberties of Englishmen secured to them by their history "from Magna Charta to the Declaration of Right . . . as an *entailed inheritance* . . . specially belonging to the people of this kingdom, without any reference whatever to any other more general or prior right" and the illusory "abstract perfection" which he saw in the "rights of men" of the French Revolution was in fact less sharp than he wanted to believe. The first Continental Congress of America on October 14, 1774, had asserted the liberties of the American colonists under the laws of nature and "the principles of the English constitution," and the Continental Congress that declared the "causes and necessity of taking up arms" on July 6, 1775, had done so "in defense of the freedom that is our birthright" as Englishmen. The debates in the National Constituent Assembly of France that proclaimed the Declaration of the Rights of Man in 1789 vividly revealed the influence of American thought; and Burke glorified the constitutional liberties of Englishmen rooted in English history at the expense of the Rights of Man of the French Revolution in an effort explicitly designed to combat the influence of the French Revolution in England. In the outcome, democracy in the nineteenth century grew more swiftly and surely in England than in France, although not so vigorously as in the United States.

In Chapter III, we noted the interaction of the Industrial Revolution with the American Revolution and the French Revolution in shaping a great divide in Western history that spanned the closing decades of the eighteenth century and the turn into the nineteenth. It is the common view that the Industrial Revolution came first to England, and the view may be accepted insofar as particular points of origin and terminus can ever be identified for complex developments in the fluid continuity of history. England was the first state to enjoy the power and profit of modern applied science and technology, as she became "the workshop of the world." English society was also the first to feel the disruptions and contortions generated by the impact of the scientific and industrial revolutions, and the first to confront the long struggle to vindicate the significance of human personality in the conditions of modern technology and industrial organization.

The Results of Machinery, a nineteenth-century booklet distributed by the Society for the Diffusion of Useful Knowledge exulted: "Two centuries ago, not one person in a thousand wore stockings; one century ago not one person in five hundred wore them; now, not one person in a thousand is without them." The booklet omitted other facts less likely to arouse feelings of triumph. The thread for the stockings was spun and the stockings were woven in squalid agglomerations of factories and hovels that swallowed up old villages and blotted the countryside. English coal and iron and the new techniques made Britain pre-eminent in the manufacture of metals and machinery. They also turned a large area of the Midlands into the Black Country. The peasantry were drained off the land into the textile slums and the Black Country of iron and coal. As the pace of expansion strained the supply of adult labor, the supply was augmented by children drawn largely from poorhouses and houses of correction. Local government in the towns, still in the rudimentary form inherited from an older village order, was hopelessly overtaxed by the new industrial growth. The conditions of the period still stand in Western history as an archetype of industrial urban wretchedness. The misery was intensified early in the nineteenth century by a depression following the end of the protracted wars with Napoleon.

The pain and the promise of the industrial transformation of England were felt in a society whose conscience was stirred by religious movements still running strongly from origins in the preceding century. The Wesleyan revival of the eighteenth century had not only produced the Methodist Church but had jolted the clergy and laity of the Church of England out of a then fashionable lethargy. The Evangelical Movement quickly extended its influence from religious doctrine to social attitudes. It roused a mood of reform in wide sectors of public opinion, and animated brilliant and tenacious leaders like the Earl of Shaftesbury and Florence Nightingale who could canalize the mood into channels of action. At the same time, the expansion of democracy increased the political means available to give effect to public concern. The composite of widening industrial experience, quickened conscience, enlarged suffrage, and personal leadership brought about a succession of remedial measures and movements.

As early as 1802 and again in 1816, statutes were enacted to ameliorate the conditions under which children worked in the factories, and they were supplemented in time by the Factory Act of 1833 which prohibited the employment of children less than nine years old in textile factories, limited the hours of work of children between nine and thirteen to forty-eight a week and nine a day, and restricted the work period of children between thirteen and eighteen to twelve hours a day and sixty-nine a week. The Factory Act of 1833 also instituted the beginnings of a system of factory inspection by paid inspectors. The conditions of manufacturing and labor were further ameliorated by the repeal of the Combinations Act in 1824, the adoption of a law in 1825 to permit workers to organize for the purpose of improving their wages and hours, the Factory Acts of 1844 and 1850, the Ten Hour Bill of 1847, and the Trade Union Act of 1871. The structure of public relief was strengthened by the Poor Law of 1834, establishing central Poor Law Commissioners to supervise the various local Boards of Guardians of the poor. Local Boards of Health were set up in 1831. The Metropolitan Police force of London was created in 1829, other municipal police forces in 1835, and a fillip was given to the establishment of county police forces by legislation in 1839. Local government received comprehensive attention in the Municipal Corporations Act of 1835, providing a modernized and uniform plan of government for boroughs and cities throughout England, with the exception of London and certain other specified communities. Educational grants-in-aid were instituted in 1833 and increased in 1839. The Bank Charter Act of 1844 required the Bank of England to separate its general banking from its note-issuing and to cover its note issues by coin or bullion and, to a specified and limited degree, government securities; and the same Act imposed limitations upon note-issuing by other banks as the beginnings of a plan that eventually confined bank notes to those issued by the Bank of England. Other illustrations can be multiplied. We turn to the consequences for British administration.

The well-born or well-connected gentlemen and retainers who held office by virtue of patronage, family solicitude, or proprietary tradition had neither the capacity nor the appetite to carry the burden of executing the regulatory measures. Men of quite another sort were needed. That was plain enough. It was much less clear that the men needed would be wanted by those who sat in the seats of political power, or that they would be available if sought. There is no automatic correspondence between the need for men able to govern and the demand for such men in governments, nor between the need for talent and its practical availability. On the contrary, the discrepancy between the qualities needed to win and hold political power and those needed to govern tends to throw the relationships between need and demand and between need and supply out of joint. Britain in the nineteenth century adjusted the discrepancy. The processes of English life generated a demand for talent in administration to match the need, made the demand politically effective, produced the men, and developed a general accommodation between the realities of political power and the imperatives of effective government.

The spirit of reform, the widening of the suffrage (carried still further in the Reform Act of 1867), the new structure of parties and party leadership, the rise of the middle class, the accelerating industrialization, the spreading scientific cast of thought accompanying the applications of science, gifted personal leadership and, we must assume, other factors growing out of the matrix of English history too subtle to be specifically identified, interacted to bring the accommodation into being. They produced the series of remedial statutes and, carrying beyond the legislation, made themselves felt in the sphere of administration.

The manufacturers and merchants chafed under the incompetence of the agencies of government with which they came most often into contact, notably the Post Office, the Excise Office, and the Customs, and mounted a barrage of protest against the mismanagement prevailing in them. Thomas Carlyle, moody and intense, a sort of minor prophet in one sector of British intellectual society, trumpeted a call for a ". . . Minister that will attack the Augias [sic] Stable of Downing Street, and begin producing a real Management, no longer an imaginary one, of our Affairs; *he,* or else in few years Chartist Parliament and the Deluge come: that seems the alternative. . . ."[5] Walter Bagehot, an analyst of English insti-

---

[5] Carlyle: *The New Downing Street,* Latter-Day Pamphlet no. 4 (London, 1858), p. 156.

tutions as he saw them in action at the seats of power in government and banking, inquired "why our public administration is not so good as, according to principle and the unimpeded effects of Parliamentary government, it should be." While the world envied British wealth and power and might well envy British parliamentary government, ". . . why is it," he asked, "that our English Government, which is beyond comparison the best of Parliamentary governments, is not celebrated through the world for administrative efficiency? It is noted for many things, why is it not noted for that? Why, according to popular belief, is it rather characterized by the very contrary?" [6]

The mercantile and manufacturing middle class, coveting a position in society to match their growing economic and political power, sought openings for their sons in fashionable occupations. Few had a more distinctive social *cachet* than service in the civil departments, so long identified with the landed gentry. Public office became a prime goal for the successful business families, and their sons began to penetrate the departments. At the outset, they found their way chiefly into the agencies immediately important to manufacturers and merchants, such as the Customs, the Excise, the Post Office, the Board of Trade, and the Indian Service. In time, they extended their ambit to the other offices of state. Coming

---

[6] Bagehot: *The English Constitution*, Chapter VI (Garden City, N.Y.: Doubleday & Co., Inc., Dolphin Books), pp. 235–6, 238.

to their posts through ambition rather than privilege, and aware of the consequence of the work for the commercial interests of their families, the new incumbents brought a new attitude and energy with them.

The seeds of administrative reform sprouted first in the India Service, organized under the British East India Company. Launched as a business venture by merchants in 1600, the company's fortunes became increasingly mixed with the affairs of the English government. By the end of the eighteenth century, its commercial activities had been supplemented by governmental responsibilities and powers, and it pursued its interests under governmental control. In the nineteenth century, its India Service offered natural opportunities to the sons of the upper middle class, who contributed to the company's early concern for efficiency in its organization and personnel. In 1806, the company founded a "college" at Haileybury to train "writers" for its civil service in India, and in 1813, all candidates for positions as writers were required to complete four terms of study at the college, culminating in an examination that was rigorous by the standards of the period. The Charter Act of 1833, which in effect completed the conversion of the East India Company from a trading concern to an administrative organ of the English government, required candidates for admission to the college, limited in number to four times the available vacancies, to qualify in a competitive examination.

The Crimean War in 1854 exposed scandals in army medical care and hospital organization that added a dimension to the growing popular sense of administrative need. The scandals were dramatized by Florence Nightingale's exertions in the inferno of the base hospitals improvised at Scutari. After the war and her return home, she did not allow England to forget. Her relentless assault upon the War Office's "tropical jungle of festooned obstructiveness, of intertwisted irresponsibilities, of crouching prejudices, of abuses grown stiff and rigid with antiquity, which for so many years to come was destined to lure reforming ministers to their doom" [7] added an impetus to the growing pressure for administrative reform.

Within the Conservative Party, Disraeli sensed the portent of administrative things to come. In 1852, he submitted to Lord Derby "a confidential memorandum drawn up, at my request by Mr. Anderson, of the Pay Office, a first-rate man of his kind, and who with Trevelyan . . . appear to me masters of administration. . . . The memorandum opens the great field of administrative reform in a practical method. I wish you to consider whether I should advert to this specific subject . . . and announce our intention of bringing forward the question . . . In my opinion, such a course would not only secure the session . . . for we should then have taken possession of the only questions which really interest the country . . ." Three years later, Disraeli returned to the theme in another note to Lord Derby, insisting that

[7] Strachey: "Florence Nightingale," in *Eminent Victorians* (New York: Garden City Books), p. 183.

administrative and departmental reform was "the subject of the age, so far as English politics are concerned, and we, fortunately, at present may have it. It will be taken by the other party if we do not appropriate it." [8]

The subject of the age was taken by "the other party," the Liberal Party into which the Whigs evolved, much as the Tories turned into the Conservatives. Lord John Russell as Prime Minister and Sir Charles Wood, his Chancellor of the Exchequer, fostered an initiative within the Treasury before Disraeli could stir his colleagues to action. In November, 1848, by a Treasury minute, they provided "that an inquiry should be instituted into the present state of the establishment of the Treasury and . . . the distribution and conduct of the business, in order that such changes may be made as may be required to secure the highest practicable degree of efficiency, combined with careful attention to economy. . . ." Responsibility for the investigation was assigned at the outset to Charles Trevelyan, an official high in the Treasury who had entered the Treasury after years of earlier experience as a writer in the India Service. Sir Stafford Northcote, in time to become a leader of the House of Commons and Chancellor of the Exchequer under Disraeli, soon joined Trevelyan as a co-director.

The Prime Minister and the Chancellor of the Exchequer were responding to the cumulative public demand, but the immediate push appears to have come from the

---

[8] Monypenny and Buckle: *The Life of Benjamin Disraeli*, I, 1432–3, 1436.

revolutions of 1848. The continental outbreaks of that year, though reflected in Ireland, had no specific counterpart in England. But English opinion had been sensitized to their meaning by the earlier Chartist agitation of 1839–40. Trevelyan was alive to "the circumstances which led up to the report of Sir Stafford Northcote and myself on the organization of the permanent Civil Service. The revolutionary period of 1848 gave us a shake, and one of the consequences was a remarkable series of investigations into public offices, which lasted for five years, culminating in the Organization Report." [9]

After five years, in November, 1853, Trevelyan and Northcote issued their General Report on "The Organization of the Permanent Civil Service." Hailed by John Stuart Mill as "one of those great public improvements the adoption of which would form an era in history," [1] it was condemned as "subversive" by London society, fearful that public offices would be filled "with the picked clever young men of the lower ranks." It was also resisted by most of Parliament. The storm of opposition quenched whatever fire there may have been in the intention of the government of the day to give effect to the recommendations through law. It confined its actions to an Order in Council, issued in 1855, creating a Civil Service Commission with limited powers and responsibilities. There the matter rested for a time.

The hesitation gave way before the prod of events and

[9] *Parliamentary Papers*, 1875, Vol. XXIII, Appendix to Second Report of the Civil Service Inquiry Commissioners, p. 100.
[1] Ibid., 1854–5, Vol. XX, p. 92.

constituencies. The concepts of civil administration formulated in the Northcote–Trevelyan Report and the
attitude animating it were progressively given effect.
Some twenty years after the halting establishment of the
Civil Service Commission, Dorman B. Eaton, a champion
of civil service reform in the United States, investigated
the British Civil Service at the request of President
Hayes. Eaton received a shrewd estimate from Trevelyan
of the alignment of forces through which the report came
to be vindicated: "Large as the number of persons who
profited by the former system of patronage were, those
who were left out in the cold were still larger, and these
included some of the best classes of our population—
busy professional persons of every kind, lawyers, ministers of religion of every persuasion, schoolmasters, farmers, shopkeepers, etc. These rapidly took in the idea of the
new institution, and they gladly accepted it as a valuable
additional privilege . . . whatever may have been the
individual sentiments of members of the House of Commons, they received such pressing letters from their
constituents as obliged them *to vote straight*." [2]

In the evolution of the career public services of England, the period from 1853 to 1870 may be identified as
the phase in which the system reached maturity. On June
4, 1870, an Order in Council prescribed the selection of
entrants into the Civil Service through competitive examination. It also enlarged and defined the supervisory

[2] Dorman B. Eaton: *Civil Service in Great Britain* (New York,
1880), App. A, 430–1.

responsibilities of the Treasury for the civil administration throughout the government, aside from the Foreign Office. The achievement of maturity did not end the
process of evolution. The public administration remained
a focus of lively attention. The structure of the Civil
Service was reviewed, clarified, extended, and readjusted
in a series of inquiries and executive actions in 1875,
1884–90, 1912–14, 1918, 1920, and 1929, and the habit
of periodic re-examination persists.

The currents of reform reached the Foreign Office later
than the general civil administration. The Foreign Office
and the Foreign Service were reconstituted more slowly
and, in respect of the social origin of their personnel,
perhaps never as fully. But they have come a long way,
and they continue to evolve. In the essentials, they are
organized along lines comparable to those of the Civil
Service, and they represent broadly the same kind of
accommodation between the conditions of political power
and the requirements of effective administration. Together, the Civil Service and the Foreign Service are a
comprehensive system of public administration with adequate internal consistency.

The system contains a number of classes of service,
defined according to the range, intellectual content,
degree of discretion, and degree of routine in their
functions. Within each class, the personnel are recruited
on the basis of merit, determined chiefly through competitive examinations. The Civil Service throughout the
Departments is subject to central control, by the Civil
Service Commission over examinations and the certifica-

tion of successful candidates, and by the Treasury through its Establishments Division over the numbers of personnel, classifications, remuneration, and conditions of service.

The division into classes is not to be confused with the subdivision of each class into grades. The Administrative, Executive and Clerical classes of the Civil Service, and the Senior Branch (or Branch A) and Branches B, C, D, and T of the Foreign Service are each divided into grades. The grades differ only in pay, rank, and responsibility. The classes of the Civil Service (and the branches of the Foreign Service) differ from one another in a deeper sense, somewhat as commissioned officers do from non-commissioned officers in the army or navy.

The several classes (or branches) are deliberately articulated into the stages of the English educational system. The candidates for each class are recruited at ages fitted to the usual terminal points of education within the schools or universities. The age limits for the Administrative Class of the Civil Service (and the Senior Branch, its counterpart in the Foreign Service) are designed for university graduates. Initially 22–24 and then 21–24, they have been altered since 1961 to 20–28 for the Administrative Class and 20–27 for the Senior Branch to permit the enlistment of personnel who have pursued advanced study or research or had outside practical experience. The age bracket for the Executive Class, 18–19, is designed for graduates of the secondary schools and the range for the Clerical Class, 16–17, for students leaving secondary school at an intermediate

THE THINGS THAT ARE CAESAR'S

stage. The age limits reflect assumptions built into the system. The candidates are picked when young for a lifetime of service, from levels of education believed appropriate to the functions of the respective classes. Their larger competence is matured through experience within the class. While individuals can bridge the gap between the Executive Class and the Administrative Class, such promotions are held to a small fraction of the higher class, in the conviction that the broad liberal education of the British universities is an essential qualification for it. Over the twelve-year period between 1923 and 1935, the entrants into the Administrative Class by promotion from below aggregated some 20 per cent of the total. In the years before World War I, the proportion was smaller.

The Civil Service also includes categories of another sort. The most numerous are the industrial employees of the arsenals, dock yards and public works, and the "minor and manipulative" personnel found chiefly in the Post Office. The most highly skilled are the professional, scientific, and technical staff. Excluding the industrial and minor and manipulative categories, the Civil Service numbers some 461,700. The Administrative Class, comprising between 2,550 and 3,600 officers,[3] constitutes no more than three fourths of one per cent of the aggregate.

[3] *Annual Abstract of Statistics* (London: Central Statistical Office; 1963), Table 138 (p. 113) reports the higher figure, but *Britain: An Official Handbook* (London: Central Office of Information; 1964) reports the lower. The discrepancy is not explained.

In the Foreign Service, the size of the Senior Branch can only be estimated, since the data are not published. A comparison of the numerical pattern of recruitment by the Administrative Class of the Civil Service and the Senior Branch of the Foreign Service in the period since World War II suggests that the total enrollment of the latter may number between one quarter and one third the membership of the former. On net impression, I should estimate the Senior Branch to number between 700 and 800. The current rate of recruitment in both remains low. The annual number of entrants into the Administrative Class in the years 1958–62 ranged from 40 to 61, and into the Senior Branch of the Foreign Service from 11 to 32. The small numbers reflect a conscious choice. "It has been the tradition, and a good tradition, that the senior Branch of the Foreign Service, like the Administrative Class of the Home Civil Service, should be small in numbers but of undeniable quality." [4]

It is the Administrative Class and the Senior Branch that have given public administration in Britain its distinctive flavor. Highly selected, educated mainly at Oxford or Cambridge, typically drawn from similar social backgrounds in the upper middle class or the aristocracy, nurtured in the same intermingled traditions of public service and assured status, and shaped in the same kind of administrative experience, their members share a common outlook and a sense of corporate identity. At

[4] Report of the Committee on Representational Services Overseas Appointed by the Prime Minister (the Plowden Committee), February 1964, p. 31.

least until the rise of the Labor Party after the First World War, the community of outlook and social origin embraced the political leadership in the Cabinet and Parliament as well as the higher career services, and fostered a ready mutual understanding and confidence between the political and the administrative sectors.

The duties of the Administrative Class "are those concerned with the formation of policy, with the co-ordination and improvement of Government machinery, and with the general administration and control of the Departments of the Public Service." [5] The "formation of policy" has its ambiguities, which could trouble a political leadership sensitive over possible intrusion into its sphere. It has raised the eyebrows of more than one commentator. Spokesmen for the Administrative Class have tried to define it.

. . . The business of government, if it is to be well done, calls for the steady application of long and wide views to complex problems: for the pursuit, as regards each and every subject-matter, of definite lines of action, mutually consistent, conformed to public opinion and capable of being followed continuously while conditions so permit and of being readily adjusted when they do not. Almost any administrative decision may be expected to have consequences which will

[5] Report of the Joint Committee on Reorganization of the National Whitley Council, 1920, repr. in White: *The Civil Service in the Modern State* (University of Chicago Press: 1930), p. 42.

endure or emerge long after the period of office of the
Government by which or under whose authority it is
taken. It is the peculiar function of the Civil Service,
and the special duty of the Administrative Class of that
Service, in their day to day work to set these wider and
more enduring considerations against the exigencies
of the moment, in order that the Parliamentary con-
venience of today may not become the Parliamentary
embarrassment of tomorrow. This is the primary justification of the permanent administrative service. . . .
The formation of policy in this limited sense—subject
always to the control of the Minister and to the supreme
authority of Parliament—is typical of administrative
work in all departments and in relation to all subject
matters whether of greater or of lesser importance.

All administrative work . . . To a large extent . . .
consists in the application to particular circumstances
of general principles laid down in the statutes, or the
administration of financial provision made by Parliament, in pursuance of the powers vested in the Department in that behalf. It involves necessarily the
preparation or study of proposals for the alteration of
the existing law in the light of changed circumstances,
new policies, or experience. It is indeed true that proposals for amending legislation within the administrative sphere do, to a large extent, and perhaps mainly,
emanate from Departments. The statement that these
processes form an important part of the work of administration affords however no ground for any suggestion that the Civil Service seeks to usurp the func-

tions of Parliament itself. The functions are essentially different.[6]

The description does not conceal some touchiness on the part of the Administrative Class concerning the nub of the business. What is the relationship between public opinion and the political leadership represented in Parliament and the Cabinet and the Administrative Class and the Senior Branch of the permanent career services? The relationship is the core of the system in terms of British constitutional tradition and prospects. It is also the heart of the matter for our inquiry into the disparities and possible accommodations between what is needed to win and hold political power and what is needed to govern.

The Administrative Class and the Senior Branch serve the ministers who are the political heads of the departments and agencies of the government. They abstain from politics; and at least as long as the Liberal and Conservative parties dominated the politics of England, shifts in party fortune placed little strain upon the political neutrality of the Civil Service and Foreign Service. The career officers give continuity to the processes of government, along with relevant general knowledge and skill, relevant specialized knowledge and expertise, and a long view detached from transient issues or political passions. They receive political direction and contact with public opinion from the ministers, who use them as an instrument to help give effect to the policies of the Cabinet and Parlia-

[6] Appendix VIII to Minutes of Evidence: Statement submitted by the Association of First Division Civil Servants to the Royal Commission on the Civil Service (1929–30).

98

ment. The ministers also shield the career officers from the cuts and blows of partisan attack or parliamentary irritation. That at any rate has been the theory. With due allowance made for the friction in any system and the normal margins of variance between the formulation of an idea and its application in practice, the theory appears to have been generally vindicated in operation during the half century between the Order in Council of June 4, 1870, and the end of World War I.

In the last few decades, the picture has become less clear, and British and American views concerning the systetm have become less uniformly sunny. The doubts that have begun to cloud public opinion run mainly in one direction. There appears to be no suspicion that the career services may again be corrupted by the old vices of political jobbery and patronage. On this score, confidence in the Civil Service and the Foreign Service remains firm, and the evidence warrants the confidence. But there is some uneasiness as to how far the Administrative Class and the Senior Branch remain instruments that really serve political leaders and public opinion expressed through Parliament, and how far they remain competent to execute policies or assist in the formulation of policies appropriate to the needs of a changing society.

There are fears in some quarters that the career services are tending toward stodginess, overemphasis upon methods that have become irrelevant or even trivial however valid they may once have been, rigidity and unadaptability. There is also some apprehension that the career services may have begun to drain the realities of political power from those properly charged with it, whether through popular elections or constitutional doctrine. There are some who resent the Administrative Class and more especially the Senior Branch of the Foreign Service as anachronistic citadels of privilege, essentially confined to personnel drawn from particular social strata in defiance of the democracy now broadening through British society. The resentment is paralleled by some belief that with the advent of the Labor Party, the old easy mutual understanding and confidence between the political and administrative sectors has given way at some points to misunderstanding and distrust.

In some respects, the fears are not new. Walter Bagehot in 1867 pointed to defects he believed inherent in a career service, in which the incumbents "are brought young into the particular part of the public service to which they are attached; they are occupied for years in learning its forms —afterwards, for years too, in applying these forms to trifling matters." He warned that if a government office is "left to itself, the office will become technical, self-absorbed, self-multiplying. It will be likely to overlook the end in the means; it will fail from narrowness of mind; it will be eager in seeming to do; it will be idle in real doing." [7] Even Sir Stafford Northcote, joint author with Charles Trevelyan of the Northcote-Trevelyan Report of 1853, publicly expressed some fear that, in certain circumstances, the administrative system could become "a bureaucratic despotism; that is to say, the permanent officials will take the management of affairs into their

[7] Bagehot: *The English Constitution*, Chapter VI, pp. 225, 230.

hands, and Parliament will have little to do, and the great mass of the people will have little to do." . . ." [8] The second Royal Commission on the Civil Service, the so-called MacDonnell Commission of 1912–14, showed concern over class barriers arising from the requirement of university training for the Administrative Class and the recruitment primarily from Oxford and Cambridge. It insisted upon maintenance of the educational requirements, but called for the elimination of the barriers through a broadened opportunity for university education. "We cannot too earnestly repeat that it is not by lowering the educational standard of the highest ranks of the Civil Service, but only by enabling the clever sons of poor parents to benefit by University training, and thereby enter the Civil Service, that the interests of democracy and of the public service can and ought to be reconciled." [9]

But if the apprehensions are not new, they have been sharpened by an awareness of contemporary facts.

Recalling Sir Earnest Satow's definition of diplomacy as the "application of intelligence and tact to the conduct of official relations between the Governments of independent States," Harold Nicolson was impressed by its current irrelevance. The definition, "adequate though it was when written, strikes us today as but a nonchalant evasion of those professional duties which modern democracy demands from its Foreign Service. . . ." Nicolson empha-

[8] In a speech in Edinburgh in 1884, reproduced in Lang: *Life, Letters and Diaries of Sir Stafford Northcote* (Edinburgh: William Blackwood & Sons, Ltd.; 1890), II, 219.
[9] Parliamentary Papers, 1914, Vol. XVI, Fourth Report of the Royal Commission on the Civil Service, p. 39.

sized the need not only for "democratization alone . . . [but for] modernization and rationalization; not only should the service become more representative of the sovereign people, but it should also correspond more effectively to modern needs." [1]

Noting that some 94 per cent of the successful candidates for appointment to the Senior Branch of the Foreign Service in the decade 1952–62 were drawn from Oxford and Cambridge, the Plowden Committee could not "regard the present situation as satisfactory either to the Foreign and Commonwealth Services or to the universities." The committee recognized that a lingering suspicion of class obstacles to entry into the Senior Branch is fed by circumstances beyond the familiar "Oxbridge" complex. In the same decade, 70 per cent of the entrants into the Senior Branch had received their secondary education in "public schools" of the Eton, Winchester, Harrow, or Rugby type. Famous for their accomplishments, the public schools are in some quarters still partly identified with an outlook satirized by Galsworthy in 1907: "I believe in my father, and his father, and his father's father, the makers and keepers of my estate, and I believe in myself and my son and my son's son. . . . And I believe in the Public Schools, and especially the Public School that I was at. And I believe in my social equals and the country house, and in things as they are, for ever and ever. Amen." [2]

---

[1] Harold Nicolson: "The Foreign Service," in *The British Civil Servant*, ed. Robson (London: G. Allen and Unwin, Ltd.; 1937), pp. 47, 56.
[2] Galsworthy: *The Country House*, Chapter VIII.

However one may evaluate Lord Chief Justice Hewart's salty attack on the Civil Service as a system "intended to produce, and in practice producing, a despotic power which at one and the same time places Government departments above the Sovereignty of Parliament and beyond the jurisdiction of the Courts," [3] it is clear that the Chief Justice was directing himself to a problem he regarded as painfully present and not in some speculative future.

The difficulties are real. Will the British adjust their public administration to fit the new democracy, the new values, and the new needs? Most observers familiar with British history and current developments will be disposed to believe that they will. Whatever the outcome, the record establishes the British experience of the past century as a brilliant accommodation between the factors through which political power is won and the conditions required for the effective conduct of government. The record also makes clear that the accommodation can only be understood in relation to the matrix of British life out of which it developed. It has been a projection of British society and values, and it offers lessons that can be useful to others only if they are read in context and applied with selective circumspection.

[3] Lord Hewart of Bury: *The New Despotism* (London: Ernest Benn, Ltd.; 1929), p. 14.

CHAPTER VI

THE PRUSSIAN-GERMAN
ACCOMMODATION

> . . . the progress of democratic institutions during
> the 19th century necessarily followed, in England, a
> course very different from that which it was to follow
> in the other countries of Europe. On the Continent the
> bureaucratic state was already in being, and nothing
> more was required than the transference to other hands
> of this pre-existent machinery and its employment for
> novel purposes. In England the machinery itself had to
> be created.
>
> Halévy, *A History of the*
> *English People, 1815–1915*

The German experience of a career administrative service is two centuries older than the English. Modern
Germany was built around Prussia, and the Prussian
state was built on three institutions: the monarchy, the
army, and the civil service. A half century before the
birth of the United States of America, the Prussian civil
administration had already evolved through several generations into a career service recruited through competitive examinations. When King Frederick William IV
granted Prussia a parliament in 1850, it had to find its
place within a structure dominated by the king, the civil
administration, and the army. There was little give in the
structure, and the way was hard. The relationship of the

fledgling Prussian Diet to the established order was illuminated in 1860–63.

In 1860, King William I of Prussia decided to enlarge the army by thirty-seven infantry and ten cavalry regiments. A bill to authorize the expansion and appropriate the necessary funds was placed before the lower house of the Diet. To the King's annoyance, the lower house presumed to examine the measure. It even offered a view of its own, stipulating that the term of enlistment for the regular army be reduced from three years to two, and that the *Landwehr,* a reserve component which the King wanted to downgrade, be retained within the field army. The King's minister altered his tactics. Withdrawing the bill, he demanded that the necessary funds be voted as a part of the general budget. The Diet swung toward acquiescence; and the impatient King began to reorganize the army in bland indifference to the absence of an authorizing statute.

New elections in December, 1861, brought a majority of progressives and liberals into the lower chamber and hardened its mood. It challenged the unauthorized reorganization, declined to appropriate funds, and called on the King to submit a detailed budget. The Diet was dissolved for its pains. When a subsequent election, in May, 1862, appeared to vindicate the progressive and liberal groups by further increasing their majority, the lower chamber took heart and renewed its demand. William I responded by calling Bismarck to his service as the King's chief minister.

Bismarck set himself single-mindedly to execute the

King's purpose, brushing aside the contentions of the recalcitrant lower house with unconcealed disdain. Upon the insistence of its members that they voiced the will of the people, he made clear his view that the people's will had nothing to do with the case. It was the duty of the legislators—so he instructed the Diet—not to represent the mistaken notions of their constituents but to correct them. He reminded the lower house that Prussian ministers, unlike English, were not responsible to Parliament but were "ministers of His Majesty, the King," and he emphasized his position in terms still indentified with his name: "not through speeches and majority decisions are the great questions of the day decided . . . but through blood and iron."

When the Diet refused to be cowed, Bismarck by-passed it. Dispensing with "majority decisions" and ignoring all speeches save his own, he proceeded to reorganize the army, spend funds as needed, and collect taxes to finance the expenditures, without benefit of parliamentary authorization or appropriation. He remained deaf to importunities and imprecations, although the lower house adopted a resolution censuring the government for unconstitutional behavior, and industrialists and jurists prayed the King to be mindful of his duty under the constitution.

For Bismarck, "the necessity that the state exists [was] enough. . . . Necessity alone [was] the determining factor." [1] Under the authority of "necessity" and the King's

[1] Pinson: *Modern Germany* (New York: The Macmillan Company; 1954), p. 129.

will, the army recruited the new regiments and paid for them out of taxes collected by the civil service. When the Diet maintained its outcry, the King's minister dissolved it again. Although a larger majority than ever was returned for the opposition in the elections of October, 1863, the King and his minister, the army, and the civil service pursued the even tenor of their way. In a contest between the Constitution of 1850 and the main constituent elements of the Prussian state, Bismarck had no fear of the outcome. The event vindicated his calculation. The populace submitted, and the taxes were paid.

Was there no John Hampden in Prussia? "True, a solitary figure like the democratic deputy Johann Jacoby vaguely suggested public refusal to pay taxes. . . ." [2] Yet in the lower house that had censured the King's minister, among the opposition that had been returned with increasing strength in successive elections, none raised his voice to support the suggestion. All stood by when Jacoby was arrested and tried for sedition.

The parallel and contrast with the case of John Hampden pique the mind and stir reflections on the nature and sources of liberty and law. In seventeenth-century England as in nineteenth-century Prussia, an imbroglio between the Crown and Parliament originated in a king's desire for money to expand his armed forces. Threatened by France in the Channel in 1634, King Charles I of England wanted more ships and crews for his navy. Scorning to summon Parliament for the funds he required, he exercised a royal prerogative to levy upon the port

[2] Ibid., p. 130.

towns for ships and upon the maritime counties for equipment, justifying the measure through the evocation of an ancient precedent. Charles soon went beyond the precedent by converting the levy from a requisition of ships into a demand for money to be used for ships. His initial demands—it must not be forgotten—were met and the money paid. Charles's needs increased, and he turned to Laud as William I later turned to Bismarck.

The Stuart king's minister showed no more scruple and no less drive than the nineteenth-century Prussian. Laud made the precedent mean what he chose it to mean. "Since it is lawful for the King to impose a tax for the equipment of the navy, it must be equally so for the levy of an army: and the same reason which authorizes him to levy an army to resist, will authorize him to carry that army abroad that he may prevent invasion. . . . Let him only abstain from war for a few years that he may habituate his subjects to the payment of that tax, and in the end he will find himself more powerful and respected than any of his predecessors." [3] The extension of King Charles's asserted authority from the navy to the army was matched by an expansion of the levy from the "ship-money" imposed only upon the port towns and maritime counties to a general tax upon the country as a whole.

Many Englishmen saw the handwriting of despotism upon the wall. A new rush of settlers to New England

[3] From a letter of Sir Thomas Wentworth, lord lieutenant of Ireland, to Laud, quoted in Green: *Short History of the English People* (New York: Sully and Kleinteich) IV, 289–90. The words were Wentworth's, but they expressed Laud's views as well as the writer's.

ensued, not unlike the emigration of Germans to America after the collapse of the Revolution of 1848. Even John Hampden appears to have bought land on Narragansett Bay as a precaution against the hazard that loomed over him.

In January, 1636, Hampden announced his celebrated refusal to pay the tax. He undertook to vindicate his defiance in the courts as well as through parliamentary and public opinion. But Charles I, confident of his support by a servile bench, privately consulted the judges of the realm and obtained an advisory opinion supporting the tax. With the favorable response safely in his hand, Charles abandoned privacy for publicity and proclaimed the judges' opinion far and wide. The prospect looked bleak, but Hampden held his ground, staking his hopes on an open trial and its possible repercussions.

The case came to trial in November and December of 1637, when the full bench heard twelve days of argument and adjourned to reach its conclusion. The court handed down its decision against Hampden in June of the following year. While a minority of two judges supported Hampden's position on the merits and three others on technical points, a majority amply vindicated Charles I's confidence in them. Chief Justice Finch was blunt and clear: "Acts of Parliament to take away the King's royal power in the defense of his kingdom are void, they are void acts of Parliament to bind the King not to command the subjects, their persons, and goods, and I say their money too, for no acts of Parliament make any difference." His fellow judge, Berkeley, was moved to wit and rhyme, insisting that he had never read or heard "that *lex* was *rex*, but it is common and most true that *rex* is *lex*." [4] And so the courts of England failed Hampden. But the case contributed its portion to the ferment in English opinion. The King's attention meanwhile was distracted by a rising of the Scots, and the opposing forces ran their course until the glorious Revolution of 1688–89 and the Act of Settlement of 1701 vindicated Hampden's position, the authority of Parliament, and the independence of the courts.

In the confrontation between King William I and the Diet in nineteenth-century Prussia, no taxpayer appears to have made a serious attempt to challenge the levy in a court of law. It is easy to assume that only fear or docility prompted the taxpayer to hold his tongue. But even apart from questions concerning the availability of judicial remedies under the Prussian law of the period, it may be doubted whether the ordinary Prussian subject believed the tax unlawful. While fear and docility played their part, his compliance may well have reflected an instinctive acceptance rooted in tradition. From the beginnings of the Prussian state and earlier in the precursor state of Brandenburg, the king's command had been the law, and his command had been made known to the subject through the king's duly established civil administration, comprising the judges along with the tax assessors and tax collectors and other civil officials. Only one other secular institution, the king's army, equaled the king's

[4] Green: *Short History of the English People*, IV, 300–1.

civil service in age, continuity, and the pervasiveness of its presence, or surpassed the civil service in prestige. Although a constitution had been adopted in 1850 and a Diet elected and assembled, a dozen years could hardly have sufficed to establish them in the thought and feeling of the society as equivalent to the king, his civil service, or his army in their claim to devotion and obedience. "Prussia [in the seventeenth, eighteenth, and the first half of the nineteenth century] was not, like France or England, a formed state, with a contiguous and homogeneous territory. . . . A steadily growing State, in a constant process of formation down to 1866, . . . A scattered State, with territories that eventually stretched from the Rhine to the Vistula, . . . There was no unity of a common tradition; there was not, until the end of the eighteenth century, the unity of a common body of law; . . . the one unity was that of a common administration. We may almost say that the Prussian State was a transcendent administrative entity (with an army at its core) superimposed on the lively and homely fact of scattered provinces and divergent provincial sentiments."[5]

The Prussian Civil Service was born in the "Holy Roman Empire's biggest sandbox," the Mark of Brandenburg, situated in north Germany between the Elbe River and the Oder. It was sired by the Elector of Brandenburg, the "Great Elector," in the travail of the Thirty Years' War and its aftermath. Brandenburg stood among some eight-

---

[5] Barker: *The Development of Public Services in Western Europe* (Oxford University Press; 1944), p. 21.

een hundred distinct political entities that collectively constituted Germany, ranging in size from the tiny domains of the "knights of the empire" to the larger countships, duchies, and principalities, and including more than sixty ecclesiastical principalities ruled by archbishops, bishops, or abbots and over fifty "free cities." In 1648, when the Treaty of Westphalia ended the agony of the Thirty Years' War, the rulers of eight German states, the Elector of Brandenburg among them, enjoyed the privilege of electing the emperor of the loose and shadowy Holy Roman Empire, mocked by Voltaire as the "body which was called and still calls itself the Holy Roman Empire" though it was "neither holy, nor Roman, nor an empire in any way."

The Thirty Years' War ravaged Germany. Ten million deaths reduced the combined population by a third. Cities were burned, farms laid waste, the structure of economic life shattered, and the peasants and workers pauperized to the point of utter destitution. Brandenburg suffered its full share. The Elector Frederick William inherited a wasteland from his father in 1640, eight years before the war dragged to an end.

Along with the disintegration wrought by the war, the Great Elector fell heir to a social order in which the landed nobility and a patrician class within the cities guarded feudal powers and privileges to a large degree independent of control by the ruler of the state. Through the ancient estates of the realm, they could veto any tax, and they customarily conditioned their consent to necessary levies upon the Elector's recognition of their estab-

112

lished position and their claims to a part of the revenue.

The feudal separatism, the general destitution and the vulnerability of Brandenburg before the armies of Sweden from the north, the Emperor from the south, and France to the west marked the horizon upon which Frederick William set his vision. Austere, ambitious, canny, and resolute, he fixed his course upon the goals of security against enemies from without and uncontested authority and order within the state. He aimed at a unitary state, strong and taut, controlled and directed from the center. He would fashion it through two instruments, an army and a civil service, but first the instruments themselves had to be made. In the forty-eight years of his reign, he brought both into being and projected the lines of their subsequent growth.

The army came first, as the expression of his initial power and the means to enhance it. He would not rest content with the kind of army that was his due under the feudal tradition, an aggregate of the separate forces of feudal lords bound to him as their overlord to come together at his call and combine under his command. The feudal lords owed him a duty of support but their forces remained bound to them, and they might discharge their duties half-heartedly or even not at all. He wanted a unified standing army, serving his will and bound to him alone. He required no gift of foresight to know how the established nobility of Brandenburg would look upon such an army. They saw its implications for their own power and status as well as the Elector's, and they opposed most strongly the features that most appealed to Frederick William. It took guile and force to break or circumvent their resistance. The Great Elector had both, and used them unsparingly toward his fixed objective.

Beginning with a nucleus of the troops under his immediate command as a feudal lord himself, the largest in Brandenburg, he augmented it by steady accretions. He played upon the animosities between the landed gentry and the urban aristocracy, upon local rivalries and family jealousies, dividing to rule in a good old-fashioned way. The landowners had not escaped the penury that crushed the peasants in the wake of the Thirty Years' War. With their agricultural labor diminished through death or dispersion, their lands untended, their livestock depleted, and the prices for such produce as they could raise depressed by the general depopulation and confusion, they went heavily into debt and mortgaged their estates. To preserve their property and former position, they needed the help of the state in the form of moratoriums upon debt or the remission of interest. The Great Elector did not miss the opportunity to turn their distress to his own purposes. In the end, he had his way, not completely but enough to bequeath a basis for consolidation by his successors.

The needs of the army determined the first functions of the civil service, to provide supplies and equipment for the army through management of the Elector's domain (land, forests, and mines held by him in his own right) and the collection of taxes. To man the civil service, the Great Elector passed over the aristocracy and recruited commoners whose interests could ride easily with his own. The internal order upon which he was bent would be a boon to them. If they felt anything at all about his gradual absorption of feudal privileges into the unified authority of the Elector, they could be expected to enjoy the discomfiture of the country Junkers and the patricians within the cities whose contempt they had felt so often. They apprehended no menace in the autocracy to which the Elector aspired, for it mattered little to them whether the absolute political power to which they were subject in any event was exercised singly by a supreme overlord or severally through the feudal nobility. They would find the unaccustomed taste of authority sweet and would glory in the sense of identification with a ruler whose prestige would in some small degree rub off on to them.

The Great Elector chose his men for the civil service where he found them, whether in Brandenburg or in other German states. He was interested only in their loyalty, obedience, and capacity to do a job, and selected them accordingly. From the outset, he organized the civil service on the pattern of unity and hierarchy toward which he shaped the army. He established a single civil service for all his territories, extending throughout the state and closely directed from the center. Tolerating no local or provincial attachments in his officials, he regularly stationed them in districts with which they had no prior connection.

Through the marriage of the Great Elector's grandfather, John Sigmund, to Anna, daughter and heiress of the

Duke of Prussia and heiress through her mother's line to ducal territories on the lower Rhine, the Hohenzollern family holdings that centered in Brandenburg had been extended to embrace East Prussia to the east and the Rhineland Duchy of Cleves and County of Mark to the west. By conquest and diplomatic maneuver in the late phases of the Thirty Years' War, the negotiation of the Treaty of Westphalia and thereafter, the Great Elector acquired Farther Pomerania to the northeast on the Baltic Sea, and the smaller states of Magdeburg, Halberstadt, and Minden to the southwest and west. In consequence, Frederick William united within himself the titles of Elector of Brandenburg, Duke of Prussia (East Prussia, West Prussia having fallen to the King of Poland in the fifteenth century), Duke of Cleves, Count of Mark, and sundry others expressing his overlordship of the other states within his inheritance. In the pursuit of his set purposes, he had to cope not only with the disintegration left by the Thirty Years' War in Brandenburg itself but also with the geographical dispersion and centrifugal dynastic loyalties of the other German states that he ruled.

In such a setting, the unitary authority, the unified army and the single civil service toward which he drove took on a dual significance. They became not only the means through which to integrate the scattered territories of the Hohenzollerns into a single state but the symbol and even the essence of the unified state.

In inaugurating the civil service and shaping the new army, he sought to instill into both an outlook expressed in the motto he adopted for his house, *"Pro Deo et populo."* To the Great Elector himself, the motto was more than mere show. It represented a commitment to the God from whom he claimed support for his authority to reign and to the people over whom he was resolved to exercise absolute dominion. When he died in 1688 after forty-eight years of unremitting effort, he left a civil service that administered internal taxes and customs, a salt monopoly, and the lands, forests, and mines of the Elector's own domain in support of the most powerful army in North Germany, as well as a postal system that helped to knit together his scattered territories.

His son and successor added nothing to the heritage of civil administration and military organization left by the Great Elector, but did score a gain in status through a diplomatic stroke. In return for his pledge of support to the Emperor in the War of the Spanish Succession, the Emperor granted him the right to assume the title of king. Since the Elector ruled Brandenburg and all but one of his other territories as states of the residual Holy Roman Empire under the suzerainty of the Emperor, the title of king could not be used for them. Alone among the Elector's dominions, East Prussia lay outside the historic reach of the Empire, and was held by the Elector as an ultimate sovereign in his own right. To the ruler of Prussia, the royal title could be granted without impropriety. In a solemn ceremony in Königsberg on January 18, 1701, he took the title of Frederick I, King of Prussia, and the territories brought together around the Electorate of Brandenburg under the rule of the House of Hohenzollern continued on their course in the history of Europe as the Kingdom of Prussia.

It was the son of King Frederick I and grandson of the Great Elector, King Frederick William I of Prussia, who renewed the work and spirit of the Great Elector, stamping his impress upon it as the second architect of the Prussian state, army, and civil administration. "If one wishes to understand the powerful tradition of personal duty and service which lends the bureaucratic system in Brandenburg-Prussia vigor and vitality as well as its ethical grandeur, it is important to appreciate this personal element in the molding of the centralized administrative system."[6]

To the themes of unity, hierarchy, authority, and commitment inherited from his grandfather, Frederick William I added professionalism and system, and he intensified the theme of commitment into a passion. He exacted the maximum of commitment from himself as the king, giving effect to the motto of *Pro Deo et populo* through his concept of the king as the "first servant of the state." The phrase was made famous by his own son and successor, Frederick the Great, but Frederick William I expressed it through a lifetime of action. From all his subjects, whatever their class or rank, he required adherence to the pattern that he imposed upon himself.

In general conception and detailed application, the structure of the state was fitted to a tightly articulated

[6] Carl J. Friedrich: "The German and the Prussian Civil Service," in *The Civil Service in the Modern State,* ed. White (University of Chicago Press; 1930), p. 385.

framework of royal authority, the army, and the civil administration. Under a General Directory, established in Berlin as the headquarters of the civil administration, Frederick William I divided Prussia into spheres of administration, each governed through an office of "War and Domains." The title reflected the emphasis upon the management of military supplies and the lands, forests, and mines held by the king as his own domain in the functions of the civil service. Under each office of War and Domains, Councillors of Taxes controlled the financial administration of groups of towns or a single large city, absorbing the historic autonomy of German cities into the unified hierarchical system.

Frederick William I more than doubled the size of the army, raising it from 40,000 to 89,000. Unlike the Great Elector who had enlisted men where he could find them, inside or outside his own realm, Frederick William I concentrated recruitment increasingly within the Kingdom of Prussia. Subdividing the kingdom into recruitment "cantons," he obliged each to furnish the manpower for a regiment. The duties of officers and men were made uniform throughout his territories and defined in written regulations. Obedience was checked through regular inspections and regular reports in writing.

In manning the civil service, Frederick William I applied explicitly and systematically the principle of selection on the basis of merit that had been implicit and still somewhat haphazard under the Great Elector. He did not leave the meaning of merit to be determined in the discretion of his subordinates, but defined it in written regulations and prescribed uniform procedures to ensure it. To qualify for the higher civil service, applicants had first to complete a course of study in a university, centering in administration, forestry, and agriculture, grouped together in the academic doctrine of the period as "cameralism." Their qualifications were then tested in entrance examinations, and the successful candidates were required to serve a probationary term in office as an added condition precedent to a definitive appointment. Once appointed, they enjoyed security of tenure and opportunities for advancement. By an ordinance issued by Frederick William I in 1722, the highest officials were required to nominate to the king the best qualified candidates to fill vacancies.

Like the Great Elector, Frederick William I recruited the civil service primarily from commoners, in an unrelenting continuation of the Hohenzollerns' campaign to subordinate the aristocracy to the supremacy of the king. He left the nobility in no doubt concerning his intentions. In the fourth year after his accession to the throne, rejecting a protest of the landed gentry against a new land tax which they denounced as ruinous to Prussia, the King exclaimed: "The country will be ruined? I cannot believe it. But I do believe that the veto power of the Junkers will be ruined. I stabilize sovereignty like a rock of bronze."[7] In the course of his reign (1713–40), the civil service acquired a corporate cohesiveness that

<hr>

[7] Quoted in F. M. Marx: "Civil Service in Germany," in *Civil Service Abroad*, ed. White *et al.* (New York: McGraw-Hill; 1935), p. 171.

stamped its members as almost a distinct social class.

In his one notable exception to the policy of confining the civil service to entrants from the middle class, he introduced a quizzical note. Generally excluded from the executive branch of the civil service, members of the nobility were nevertheless admitted to the judicial branch, along with *"Die dummen Deuffel"* ("the dumbbells"). The designation was the King's own. We are left to guess how far the mockery reflected the King's opinion of the nobility or the judiciary, or just a passing whim.

The nobility were admitted to service as officers of the army. In fact, the rank of officer was open only to them, and they had no choice but to accept a commission offered. In effect, Frederick William I conscripted the nobility as he did the peasants and the middle class, and as he conscripted himself. In compensation for their compulsory lifetime service under his command, he recognized and confirmed their elevated social status. The theme of hierarchy prevailed in society as it did throughout the Prussian state.

The King also applied the principles of conscription and thorough training as a condition to high office to his son and heir, Frederick. Given in his youth to the French language and literature, attitudes popular in the French Enlightenment, and an outspoken admiration of Voltaire, Frederick dared to assert a measure of independence, declining to jump at his sire's bidding. Once he even sought freedom in flight. To bring the young man to heel, the King imprisoned him until he avowed an unquestioning submission to the father's command. The King rubbed the lesson in, putting Frederick through severe courses of training in administration and the army, and compelling him to marry a princess of Brunswick for whom the young man felt only aversion. When Frederick succeeded to the throne of Prussia in 1740 as King Frederick II, he had been molded in his father's pattern.

Frederick II won his epithet, the Great, through military conquests and artful diplomacy that added Silesia and West Prussia (except for Danzig and Thorn) to the territory of Prussia, along with smaller acquisitions. Prussia stood revealed as a major force in Europe, that could survive the Seven Years' War against an alliance of Austria, Russia, and France. The survival was not the doing of Frederick and Prussia alone, as some chroniclers might want to believe. Prussia was aided by the simultaneous embroilment of France in war with England in North America and India; by English subsidies provided by Pitt; and by vacillations in Russian policy generated by the illness and subsequent death of the Czarina and the known sympathies of her son and successor toward Frederick. Frederick's brilliance and the force of Prussian arms nevertheless could not be denied. His erstwhile foes saw the advantages of coming to terms with him, as Austria and Russia later did in a three-way partition of Poland.

Frederick had extended his power through his armies, but he had to digest his gains and govern his new territories. To this end, he turned to the other of the monarchy's primary instruments. His civil service moved in to Silesia and West Prussia, organized them in its own pattern and consolidated the new areas of administration into the integrated Prussian service.

While maintaining the vigor of his administrative inheritance, Frederick the Great refined and sophisticated its structure and procedures. The standards and methods of recruitment and promotion took the form that has been maintained in essence ever since. The Higher Civil Service was sharply differentiated from the Middle and Lower Services, each being assigned its own sphere and its own criteria of admission, selection, and training. Open only to university graduates, the Higher Civil Service could not be reached by promotion from the others. The prescribed course of university training was gradually changed from "cameralism" to law in the wide German academic sense, comprising elements of political theory, legal philosophy, economics, history, and penology, along with a study of statutes, decrees, and other authoritative expressions of law, never codified prior to the end of Frederick II's reign. Frederick II instituted the preparation of the first comprehensive Prussian Code, finished and published in 1791, five years after his death.

After completion of the required university course, a candidate for the Higher Civil Service had to qualify in competitive written and oral examinations. If he passed, he entered upon a probationary term of service, under the critical eye of the agency to which he was assigned. Thereafter, on the condition of a favorable recommendation from the agency, he underwent a second state examination before a supreme national examining commission, established by Frederick II in Berlin in 1770. If he survived, he was admitted to the last lap of the qualifying course through appointment as an "assessor," occupying an official position and performing official work while still subject to dismissal in the discretion of his superiors. If deemed satisfactory as an assessor, he could cross the border into his promised land as a Councilor of War and Domains, the first rung on the ladder of the Higher Civil Service, with a lifetime prospect of secure tenure before him.

Under Frederick the Great, the corporate solidarity of the Higher Civil Service increased. Warmed by a radiation of status from the Crown, it took on still more of the attributes of a separate social class, intermediate between the general middle class and the aristocracy. While the middle class remained the primary source of recruitment, the base tended to narrow under a tendency to enroll the sons and nephews of officials. The officer ranks of the army remained a preserve of the aristocracy, still under compulsion to serve, and explicitly designated "the foremost class in the State" by the King.

The austere tradition of service remained pervasive. As "the first servant of the State," Frederick the Great formulated a doctrine that the king must conduct himself at all times as if he were fully accountable to his subjects, but he tolerated no romantic notion that the kingly duties implied any corresponding rights of the subject. Like his father and great grandfather, he identified the state with the monarchy and the monarchy with absolute power, exercised through the king's two primary instruments, the civil service and the army. Through the army and the officer-Junker class, the king maintained and enhanced his power. Through the civil service, he governed Prussia.

The momentum imparted by Frederick the Great carried Prussia along, until disaster struck on the battlefields of Jena in 1806. Impervious to the ideas of the French Revolution, the Prussian monarchy, the army, and the civil service long prevented its seeds from sprouting on Prussian soil. But the revolutionary force, gathered up and concentrated in Napoleon, shattered the Prussian army and humbled the Prussian King. In the Peace of Tilsit, imposed on Prussia by Napoleon in 1807, the state lost its territories west of the Elbe and much of its land east of the Oder, and shrank to the compass of Brandenburg, Pomerania, Silesia, and old East and West Prussia narrowly defined.

A revolution ensued in Prussia, of a special Prussian kind. In its first phase, identified with the names of Stein and Hardenberg in the civil government and von Scharnhorst in the army, it was "a revolution not directed against the administration, but achieved by it; a revolution which left absolutism almost intact, but increased the efficiency of its methods of government. . . ."[8] Three decades were yet to elapse before the standards of liberty, the rights of man and government through the consent of the governed, unfurled in the French and

[8] Barker: *The Development of Public Services in Western Europe*, p. 24.

American revolutions, would be raised by a popular movement in Prussia. Baron vom Stein, a former Prussian civil servant, Prince Hardenberg, and General von Scharnhorst had no truck with such notions. But they did appreciate the unity, fervor, and national drive engendered in France by the Revolution. "Your Majesty," wrote Hardenberg to King Frederick William III of Prussia, "we must do from above what the French have done from below!"

The revolution from above was deliberate and systematic. "It is an illusion to think that we can resist the revolution effectively by clinging more closely to the old order, by proscribing the new principles without pity. This has been precisely the cause which has favored the revolution and facilitated its development. The force of these principles is such, their attraction and diffusion is so universal, that the state which refuses to acknowledge them will be condemned to submit or to perish . . . our guiding principle must be a revolution in the better sense, . . . the elevation of humanity through the wisdom of those in authority and not through a violent impulse from within or without." [9]

The aims of the leaders were the regeneration of Prussia and the unification of Germany through Prussia. Whatever integration of Germany there had been in the Holy Roman Empire had vanished in the Thirty Years' War, and even the ghost of the Empire had been laid by Napoleon when he formally proclaimed its termination

[9] Prince Hardenberg, quoted in Pinson: *Modern Germany*, p. 33.

in 1806. The means were a series of measures to instill in the Prussian populace a sense of identification with the civil service and the army as well as the king, and to improve the efficiency of the civil and military administration.

To stimulate the "intelligence and will of all for the support of the government," Stein and Hardenberg prevailed on the King to liberate the Prussian peasants from serfdom and make it possible for them to become free owners of parts of the land they had tilled. To the same end, a modicum of municipal self-government was restored. The towns remained under the control of the civil service, but provision was made for locally elected bodies to share responsibility with the career administrators. The civil service gained in vitality at the points of local application through the municipal reform and more broadly from the general revival of spirit, but its structure and functions remained essentially unchanged. On the military side, under the leadership of Scharnhorst, stirred by the French revolutionary concept of a "nation in arms," the army was transformed into a national army through the introduction of universal military conscription (modeled on the *levée en masse* of the French Revolution) and the exclusion of foreigners. In harmony with the amelioration in status of the peasants, the flogging of soldiers, a means of discipline practiced as a hereditary right by the officer-nobility class, was abolished.

The revolution from above did not entirely forestall a revolution from below. The spores scattered by the winds

THE THINGS THAT ARE CAESAR'S

of the French Revolution and the American Revolution did germinate among the middle class and labor sectors of the German populace in the uprisings of 1848. Starting in the South German States, they spread to the Prussian Rhineland and then to Berlin itself. While not wholly unsuccessful—it left a legacy upon which the Weimar Republic drew seventy years later—the Revolution of 1848 was snuffed out quickly, despised as a failure by the forces that crushed it, and accepted as a failure by its own proponents. The Prussian monarchy turned again to a revolution from above. The Constitution of 1850 was drafted by King Frederick William IV's own ministers and civil servants, enacted by the King, and presented for acceptance to a Diet (parliament) convened on the basis of a three-class franchise in accordance with the terms of the Constitution itself.

Prussia thus at last received a parliament, but one organized on lines reminiscent of the medieval estates. An upper house, the *Herrenhaus*, consisted of representatives of the landed aristocracy, members named by the king for life or as hereditary members, and representatives of the universities and the larger cities. The lower chamber purported to represent all citizens, at least those who paid taxes. But its members were chosen by "electors," themselves elected by the voting taxpayers, organized in three sectors according to the amount of taxes paid, *i.e.*, their wealth. Class I, the richest, contained 3.8 per cent of the voters; Class II, 13.9 per cent of the voters; and Class III, the poorest, 82.3 per cent. Each class chose one third of the "electors," who in turn elected the deputies of the lower house. The dilution of representative democracy was plain enough on the surface of the Constitution, but the underlying weakness was even more painful. As the confrontation between the Diet and the king in 1860–63 revealed, the Diet itself rested on the surface of the Prussian state, still dominated by the king and his traditional instruments, the army and the civil service.

As the liberal and democratic elements among the German people lost heart, their numbers were depleted by a flood of emigration to the United States. In the decade after 1850, Germans left to seek a new future in America at a rate of 90,000 a year, among them many of the ablest and most deeply committed proponents of democracy and freedom.

In Prussia itself, the energies of the state were concentrated upon the twin purposes of Prussian hegemony and the unification of Germany. Bismarck used the expanded army, organized in disregard of the Diet, in three critical wars against Denmark in 1864, Austria in 1866, and France in 1871. Through his victories, imaginative diplomacy, and adroit internal politics, he united Germany around Prussia. In a ceremony in the Hall of Mirrors at Versailles on January 18, 1871, King William I of Prussia was proclaimed Emperor William I of Germany, and the Second Reich (in the assumed sequence, the Holy Roman Empire was taken to be the first) was born. In the German Empire as in the Kingdom of Prussia, the king-emperor remained *der Träger der Staatsgewalt*, the bearer of the power of the state.

While the trends generated in the French Revolution and the American Revolution made slow headway in Germany, the Industrial Revolution moved apace. Although an element of arbitrariness is inescapable in assigning definite beginnings and endings to so complex and protracted a historical process as the Industrial Revolution, we may accept the general identification by historians of the decade of the 1850's as the *"erste Gründerzeit"* (first foundation time) and the 1870's as the *"Gründerjahre"* (foundation years). Making itself felt in Germany decades after it pervaded the life of Britain, the Industrial Revolution converted Germany during the Second Reich (1870–1918) from a mainly agricultural to a predominantly industrial society.

Sensitive to the social and potential political implications, mindful of the dangers revealed in the Revolution of 1848 and perhaps recalling the philosophy of Hardenberg and Stein in the years after Jena, Bismarck resumed the revolution from above. Where England in the early nineteenth century had to adjust to the industrialization of British life while it was creating an appropriate administrative instrument, Bismarck had the Prussian-German civil service ready to hand. As in the past when directed by a ruler who knew what he wanted, the civil service proved itself up to the new tasks of government.

Bismarck knew what he wanted. "For fifty years we have been talking about the social question. . . . I am not of the opinion that the principles of *laissez-faire, laissez-aller, pure Manchestertum* . . . can be applied in the paternalistic monarchical state. . . . Call this socialism, if you will, I do not care. . . ." [1] In November, 1881, comprehensive labor legislation was enacted; a health insurance law in 1883; an accident insurance law in 1884; and an old-age pension act in 1889. The "paternalistic monarchical State" continued to pursue social measures after William II, the last of the Hohenzollerns, fell out with Bismarck and in 1890 "dropped the pilot." A Law for the Protection of Labor in 1891 prescribed safety and health conditions within industry, days off for laborers on Sundays and legal holidays, protective restraints upon the employment of women, and restrictions on child labor looking toward subsequent abolition. In 1911, three years before the Second Reich descended into the pit of World War I in which it expired, a Federal Insurance Law consolidated and amplified much of the earlier legislation.

Here was a renewed application of the *"Pro Deo et populo"* that the Great Elector had made the motto of the Hohenzollern line. The King-Emperor of Prussia-Germany through his minister-chancellor chose to act as the "first servant of the State," as did Frederick William I and Frederick the Great before him. Toward the end of a century of expanding popular government in western Europe and North America, the German monarchy adopted government for the people, while still abjuring government of the people and by the people.

I have pointed to the disadvantages suffered by Britain in its encounter with the Industrial Revolution before

---

[1] Quoted in Reinhardt: *Germany: Two Thousand Years* (New York: Frederick Ungar Publishing Co.; 1961), II, 616–7.

and during the development of its civil administration. But the timing had its compensations. Emerging when it did, the British Civil Service was molded to fit the conditions of parliamentary democracy and personal freedom to which Britain remains committed. The German Civil Service, instituted by an autocrat in the seventeenth century, evolved as the instrument of a monarchy that ruled with absolute power until the middle of the nineteenth century and largely embodied the power of the state down to 1918. In England, common social origins and a common education fostered an easy concord between the political leadership and the civil service. The power of the German king—and the subordinate and supporting power of the officer-nobility caste—was articulated with the civil service through authority, obedience, and habitual deference rooted in the hierarchy of classes and reverence for the Crown.

With the end of the Prussian-German monarchy in 1918, the king ceased to be "the bearer of the power of the state." In constitutional theory, he was replaced by the sovereign people. *"Die Staatsgewalt geht vom Volke aus"* ("The power of the state emanates from the people").[2] In operation, his place was taken successively by the parliament, chancellor and ministers, and president of the Weimar Republic; Hitler; and the parliament, chancellor and ministers, and president of the Federal Republic of Germany.

[2] Constitution of the German Reich, 1919, Art. I. Art. 20 of the Basic Law of the Federal Republic of Germany, 1962, contains an identical provision, except that the initial word, "The," is replaced by "All."

The Weimar Constitution and statutes took for granted that the civil service would be necessary and appropriate for the republic and retained it in the historic pattern. The National Civil Service Act of 1873 had consolidated the inherited law and practice of the civil service. The Weimar Republic largely re-enacted it, with changes in the main no more significant than the modifications made from time to time during the Second Reich. "When in 1919 the Constitutional Convention assembled in Weimar to take stock of what was left of Germany after an exhaustive [*sic*] war that ended in revolution, the civil service had nothing to fear. On the contrary, it found itself courted by nearly all those political groups which were united in the desire for immediate reconstruction of the Reich . . . the merits of civil service, in the judgment of administration-minded people, had successfully stood the test of practical experience for generations. . . ."[3]

There was one radical departure from prior doctrine and practice. Career officials were welcomed into elective politics, along with the military. Under Article 39 of the Constitution, "Civil servants and members of the armed forces need no leave to perform their duties as members of the national assembly or of a state assembly. If they become candidates for election to these bodies, leave shall be granted them for the amount of time which is necessary to prepare for their election."[4] Civil servants

[3] F. M. Marx: "Civil Service in Germany," in *Civil Service Abroad,* p. 196.

133

accepted the invitation, constituting at times as much as one quarter of the membership of the *Reichstag* (the national assembly). Needing "no leave for the performance of their duties as members of the national assembly," they served without financial loss, receiving their regular compensation and perquisites. "For the first time in the history of German administration," a regime set aside "the tradition of rigid nonpartisanship." [5]

The motives were pure. The new German leadership appears to have thought Article 39 an unavoidable logical consequence of the principle of equal civic rights for all. To the American mind, the notion seems perversely doctrinaire. The manning of administrative posts by officials who engage in party politics is hardly unfamiliar to Americans. We may acknowledge that no inherent contradiction exists between performing the duties of such a post and partisan political activity. But that is beside the point. There is a critical inconsistency between partisan political activity and the performance of the duties of such a post by a career official with life tenure. As a permanent civil servant, he must stand ready to execute the policies of any government that comes to power through constitutional processes, and do so with the full confidence of the government. In the swings of political fortune, a career civil servant who is politically involved will in time owe allegiance to a government

[4] Carl J. Friedrich: "The German and Prussian Civil Service," in *The Civil Service in the Modern State*, p. 396.
[5] F. M. Marx: "Civil Service in Germany," in *Civil Service Abroad*, p. 252.

representing an opposing party. Although it is perhaps not inconceivable that he might achieve sufficient detachment to carry out such a government's policies in good faith, it is at least improbable. In any event, he certainly will not enjoy the confidence of the government in his objectivity and dependability, not to say fidelity. If a policy of administration through officials engaged in partisan politics is to be tenable, the officials must expect removal when an opposing party comes to power.

Difficulties could have been anticipated under the best of circumstances, and the circumstances of Germany after World War I were not the best. The bitterness of defeat, the sense of isolation from a hostile world, the sullenness of unrepentant officers, and the rise of the Communist and Nazi parties created strains beyond the capacity of the infant republic. The involvement of civil servants in electoral politics and parties did not stop short of the Nazis and Communists. When Minister Walter Rathenau was assassinated in 1922, the horrified Reichstag enacted a special act requiring the career official "to stand by the constitutional republican form of government in his official activities. He must abstain from all activities which cannot be reconciled with his position as a servant of the Republic." [6] Neither politics nor administration improved, but the evidence is too confused to warrant a verdict against the civil service. In the bewilderment and turmoil of the beleaguered republic, the misbehavior of civil servants could not be segregated from the general disintegration.

[6] Ibid., p. 256.

From the novelty of adjustment to a callow parliamentary democracy, the civil service passed under the sway of Hitler. The Fuehrer used it, although not without distaste. Early in his regime, he acknowledged the need to govern through other men than the Brown Shirts with whom he forced his way to power. The acknowledgment was traumatic, and wholly Hitlerian. In June, 1934, he shattered the leadership of his Storm Troops. Ernst Roehm and scores of Hitler's other brethren in the Nazi upsurge were suddenly shot at the Fuehrer's orders in a purge that shook Germany. In a speech to the Reichstag on July 13, 1934, Hitler explained his action. He had performed emergency surgery to save the body politic from "revolutionaries who in 1918 were shaken in their former relation to the State and became dislocated and thereby lost every inner relationship to a regulated human order of society. They became revolutionaries who . . . would like to see a continuous state of revolution. . . . Unable really to cooperate in work with anybody, . . . filled with hatred against every authority, their restlessness can only find satisfaction in . . . conspirative deed for destroying whatever at a given moment exists. . . . Achievements that seem to consolidate the new German State arouse their greater hatred . . . they do not see before them the German people but only the hated institution of order . . . in every attempted revolt, they constitute a nucleus of followers until such time as a new order of things begins to crystallize from the chaos of clashing forces. . . ." [7]

[7] *The New York Times,* July 14, 1934, p. 4.

Hitler's passions were personal power and national conquest. To them he subordinated all else, but he also had to govern. He had proclaimed a National Socialist Revolution, in a complex industrial society long accustomed to paternal direction from the regime. To govern in such a society, he turned to the organized career service inherited from the Prussian-German monarchy through the Weimar Republic. He did so despite his dislike of the elements of German life with which the civil service was identified. He believed it "impossible for a normal intelligence to understand any part of the edifices built up by the jurists. . . ." He warned his lieutenants that "Above all, it was essential that the Party should not allow itself to be overrun by the bourgeois." [8] He felt similar distrust and contempt for the "upper strata of society. Otto Meissner who was State Secretary in the office of the Presidency from the end of World War I through World War II [himself an instance of civil service continuity] quotes Hitler as saying that Lenin and Stalin had been right in annihilating the upper classes in Russia and that he, Hitler, had made a mistake in not doing likewise. After July 20, 1944, Hitler tried to correct this 'mistake.'" [9] Yet he retained the civil service, because he had to do so.

He undertook to bludgeon it into a shape that suited his purposes. Its tradition of service was corrupted into a

[8] *Hitler's Secret Conversations*, tr. Norman Cameron and R. H. Stevens from the *Bormann-Vermerke* of Martin Bormann (New York: Farrar, Straus; 1953), pp. 110, 304.
[9] A. W. Dulles, *Germany's Underground* (New York: The Macmillan Company; 1947), p. 14 n.

requirement of subservience. Its members were ordered to regard themselves as "soldiers in plain clothes." He purged its ranks according to the familiar Nazi criteria. In a grimly ironic reminder of the Weimar Republic's special legislation ordering each civil servant "to stand by the constitutional republican form of government in his official activites," Hitler fixed it as an essential condition of tenure that a civil servant "will at all times fully identify himself with the State of the National Revolution." [1]

From the Fuehrer's "Third Reich" and World War II, the civil service passed into the structure of the Federal Republic of Germany. (Its status in the "German Democratic Republic" established in the former Soviet Zone in East Germany is another story.) The Federal Republic adhered to the Weimar Republic's conviction that the principle of equal civic rights entitled career officials to run for elective office on party slates. The Constitution of 1962 provided in Article 48 that "No one may be prevented from accepting and exercising the office of deputy. He may not be dismissed from employment, with or without notice, on this ground."

The dangers revealed by the Weimar experience did receive some acknowledgment in the new Constitution. Article 137 empowers the *Bundestag* (National Assembly) in its discretion to curtail the "right of civil servants, of salaried employees of the public services, of professional soldiers, of temporary volunteer soldiers and of

[1] F. M. Marx: "Civil Service in Germany," in *Civil Service Abroad*, p. 266.

judges to stand for election in the Federation, in the *Laender* or in the communes. . . ." The *Bundestag* has shown no eagerness to apply the power reserved to it. Article 53 of the Civil Service Act enjoins civil servants and professional soldiers to pursue political activity with "moderation and restraint befitting the office," and the civil servant can no longer remain on active duty (with full pay) while serving in parliament. There the matter rests.

A clash of Anglo-American and German concepts appears to have yielded the limited qualifications upon the political privileges of civil servants. In the proceedings preparatory to the adoption of the Constitution of 1962, the Allied Military Governors had recommended a provision explicitly requiring political neutrality for civil servants. To their astonishment, the German Parliamentary Council had rejected the proposal as "foreign to German legal thought," [2] and stood its ground. The Allied representatives could not swallow Article 48 standing alone, and Article 137 was adopted to resolve the impasse.

The conditions in which the Federal Republic of Germany was launched, if perhaps less exacting than in the case of the Weimar Republic, were by no means auspicious. The aftermath of defeat and devastation in World War II, the moral and practical debris of Nazism, the tensions arising from the partition of Germany, and the geographical position of the state were burden enough. But the Federal Republic has had the gift of able

[2] *Maunz-Durig Grundgesetz Kommentar*, p. 137–2.

political leadership and the benefit of understanding and farsighted policies on the part of its erstwhile enemies to the West. There appears to be much that is hopeful in its accomplishment thus far with its new parliamentary institutions and its attempt to restore the morale and standards of the civil service. But its experience has been too brief and involved with too many cross-currents to warrant any but a tentative and qualified appraisal.

From the accession of the Great Elector in 1640 to the abdication of William II in 1918, the civil service of Brandenburg-Prussia-Germany stood out as a primary part of the state. It was internally consistent, and externally in harmony with the army whose evolution ran parallel to its own and the monarchy of which it was a vital organ. In its relation to the king and the officer-nobility caste, it constituted as remarkable an accommodation between the exigencies of political power and the requirements for the conduct of government as the British Civil Service in relation to Parliament and the Cabinet of Britain. But there is a long row to hoe before conclusions can be reached concerning the kind and degree of change that may be required to adapt the German Civil Service to the conditions of freedom and parliamentary democracy.

CHAPTER VII

SPOILERS AND REFORMERS
THE FOUNDING FATHERS
ANDREW JACKSON

God looks after fools, drunkards and the United
States of America.

Anonymous

Now, when the flame they watch not towers
  About the soil they trod,
Lads, we'll remember friends of ours
  Who shared the work with God.

Housman, A Shropshire Lad, I

1

SPOILERS AND REFORMERS

James Abram Garfield, sometime farm boy, canal barge-
man, teacher of Greek and Latin at the Western Reserve
Eclectic Institute at Hiram, Ohio, and Brigadier General
of Volunteers at Shiloh and Chickamauga, doffed his
uniform for a seat in Congress in December, 1863, as
Representative from the Ashtabula District of Ohio.
Rising swiftly to influence among the Republicans in the
House, he took part as an insider in the inauguration of

Grant on March 4, 1869. The swarm of job-seekers depressed him. "The rush for office is absolutely appalling; it would almost seem that the adult population of the United States had moved on the works of the government and were determined to carry every position by storm." [1] As he climbed the ladder of power, the swarm clustered more densely about him and stung through the politician's cloak of resigned or cynical acceptance. When Grant gave way to Hayes after two slovenly terms in the White House, and the Forty-fifth Congress assembled in 1877, Garfield emerged as the leader of the Republican Party in the House. He had "hardly arrived" at the Capitol "before the doorbell began to ring and the old stream of office-seekers began to pour in. They had scented my coming and were lying in wait for me like vultures for a wounded bison. All day long it has been a steeple-chase, I fleeing and they pursuing." [2] A knell of unwitting prophecy rang through his lament. On March 4, 1881, Garfield succeeded Hayes as President of the United States. On the 13th of June he complained: "My day is frittered away by the personal seeking of people, when it ought to be given to the great problems which concern the whole country. Four years of this kind of intellectual dissipation may cripple me for the remainder of my life." [3] Barely three weeks later, on July 2, 1881, as

[1] From a letter of March 27, 1869, in T. C. Smith, *Life and Letters of James A. Garfield* (New Haven: Yale Univ. Press; 1925), I, 446.

[2] From a letter of May 29, 1877 to Mrs. Garfield, ibid., II, 654.

[3] Ibid., II, 1151–52; a journal entry of June 13, 1881.

Garfield entered the old Baltimore and Potomac Railroad station in Washington on his way to a commencement at Williams College, he was shot by Charles J. Guiteau, one of the hungry horde, presumably deranged and seeking to avenge the frustration of his quest for office.

A storm of public outrage against political jobbery and corruption gathered while Garfield lay wounded for eighty days, and burst upon the Congress when the President died on September 19, 1881. Its fury drove politicians into an alignment with George William Curtis, Carl Schurz, Dorman B. Eaton, and the National Civil Service Reform League. By a majority of 38 to 5, the Senate passed the Pendleton Civil Service Bill in December, 1882, and the House followed suit by a margin of 155 to 47. When President Arthur, who succeeded Garfield from the Vice Presidency, signed the measure on January 16, 1883, he was not visibly embarrassed by the irony of his role.

In his politician's progress, Arthur had served for seven years as the Collector of Customs of the Port of New York, a post that enjoyed a vivid and merited reputation as a showpiece of the spoils system. When President Hayes in 1877, aiming at Civil Service reform, made the New York Custom House and Arthur his first target, Arthur railed against the injustice of punishing him for the condition of an Augean stable that he had taken and kept as he had found it. While not pretending to any attempt to cleanse the Custom House, Arthur insisted in vindication of his honor that he had not increased the volume of the prior accumulation. In

defiance of Senator Roscoe Conkling and other "Stalwarts" of the Republican Party in New York who rushed
to Arthur's support, President Hayes removed him in
1878. The Stalwarts nursed their rage and came to the
Republican Convention in 1880 with blood in their eyes.
They had had their fill of President Hayes's attempt to
restore a measure of presidential authority in the face of
the Congressional dominance that had prevailed since
the Civil War, nourished on the impeachment and near
removal of President Johnson and the submissiveness of
President Grant. They wanted an end to liberal and
reforming tendencies within the Republican Party.

Rallying behind a proposed new term for Grant, they
tried to nominate him as an instrument for their return
to unchallenged power. Stopped by a deadlock among
Grant, Blaine, and John Sherman, they were forced to
accept Garfield, who was obliged in turn to take Arthur as
the nominee for Vice President in a gesture of party
harmony. The harmony, such as it was, gave way immediately following the election to the dissonance of a
struggle between Senator Conkling and President Garfield over patronage in New York, in which Vice President Arthur unabashedly joined the Senator against the
President.

To the Civil Service reformers, Arthur symbolized the
cynicism and jobbery against which they fought. Their
horror at the assassination of Garfield was matched by
their forebodings over the succession by Arthur. His was
the hand and pen that completed the enactment of the
Pendleton Bill into the Civil Service Act of 1883.

The Act marked a triumph for a small and distinguished band—Jenckes, Curtis, Schurz, Sumner, Trumbull, Eaton, Wheeler, Bonaparte—who had energized a drive toward Civil Service reform and formulated its themes. The drive had begun immediately after the Civil War, spearheaded by Congressman Thomas Allen Jenckes of Rhode Island. Jenckes assaulted the citadels of patronage under the banner of economy. As chairman of a Joint Select Committee on Retrenchment, he introduced a Civil Service bill in the House in 1867, supported by a report of the Committee stressing the savings to be effected by a reorganization of the "subordinate civil service" to provide for the screening of candidates by examinations and appointments on the basis of merit. His bill failed to pass, but the narrow margin of the loss, 66 to 72, measured the scale of support generated by his tenacity and eloquence and the gathering organization of the reform movement among the citizenry. Although the opposition defeated Jenckes in his bid for re-election in 1870, the momentum of his labors carried through Grant's first administration and the Forty-first Congress. A rider to a civil appropriation bill introduced by Senator Lyman Trumbull of Illinois became the Act of March 3, 1871, authorizing the President to "prescribe such rules and regulations for the admissions of persons into the civil service of the United States as will best promote the efficiency thereof, and ascertain the fitness of each candidate . . . ; and for this purpose the President is authorized to employ suitable persons to conduct . . . inquiries . . . and to establish regulations for the con-

145

duct of persons who may receive appointments in the civil service." [4]

Grant employed "suitable persons" who came to be known collectively as the Civil Service Commission. Whether in a mood of weariness under the presidential burden of distributing patronage or in a tribute to the political power of the reformers, Grant designated George William Curtis, widely acknowledged by the champions of the reform movement as their leader, as the chairman of the Commission. If some observers were astonished by the appointment, it occasioned no surprise when Curtis fell out with the President and resigned in 1873. Still disposed to give representation to the reform movement, Grant designated Dorman B. Eaton, a friend and colleague of Curtis, as the latter's successor. But the Commission was too tender a plant to survive in the weedy soil of the period. Ever deferential to his acknowledged political masters in the Republican majority in Congress, Grant placed the question of continued civil service reform before the Congress in his message of December, 1874, making clear his unwillingness to carry on under exclusively presidential responsibility in the absence of specific congressional action.

Congress wanted no part of the hot potato. The opponents of the Act of March 3, 1871, confirmed their opposition, and its supporters in the main seemed to feel the Act was as far as they cared to go. When Congress adjourned without action, Grant by an order of March 9,

[4] Act of March 3, 1871, 16 Stat. 514, Rev. Stat. Sec. 1753.

1875, administered a quietus to the work of the Commission. While the Act of 1871 and the presidential authority under it were not repealed, it lapsed into disuse, inanimate though technically alive. Grant's view of its effective demise had a charm of its own. It gratified him that "civil service reform is growing in America, in the only way it can grow naturally . . . through the long continuance of one party in power, and the consequent education of an experienced class of public servants. . . . The way to achieve the best civil service is, first to influence Congressmen, and induce them to refrain from pressure upon the Executive; then pass laws giving each office a special tenure; then keep the Republican party in power until the process of education is complete. As it is now, the only danger I see to civil service is in the triumph of the Democratic party." [5]

The Jenckeses, the Curtises, the Schurzes, the Eatons saw other dangers to civil service reform. They declined to be comforted by Grant's satisfaction or to acquiesce in the lapse of the Act of 1871, and stuck to their course of pressure and persuasion. To the theme of economy set by Congressman Jenckes and the theme of efficiency, in the sense of a disciplined execution of orders and a clean dispatch of the routine business of the government, they added a deeper motif. As George William Curtis put it:

These doctrines and practices [of political jobbery] threatened popular government itself. The "spoils" system introduced by President Jackson, which is now

[5] J. R. Young: *Around the World with General Grant* (New York: 1879), II, 267–8.

stigmatized as the "American system," imperils not only the purity, economy, and efficiency of the administration of the Government, but it destroys confidence in the method of popular government by party. It creates a mercenary political class, an oligarchy of stipendiaries . . . which controls parties with relentless despotism, imposing upon them at the elections issues which are prescribed not by the actual feeling and interest of the country but solely by the necessities and profit of the oligarchy, while, to secure this advantage, party-spirit, the constant and mortal peril of republics, is inflamed to the utmost. It is a system which, by requiring complete servility to the will of the oligarchy . . . destroys the individual political independence which is the last defense of liberty . . . Government by the people, four-fifths of whom simply vote for the ticket or the measures prepared by the oligarchy, sinks practically into the empire of a corrupt ring.[6]

The reformers stressed the theme of moral regeneration as they pushed their campaign through the administration of Hayes and the abortive presidency of Garfield to their triumph in the Pendleton Act of 1883.

For two decades at least, the theme dominated the programs of the Civil Service Commission established under the Act. When Theodore Roosevelt was appointed a commissioner in 1889, he intensified the moral em-

[6] Eaton: *Civil Service in Great Britain* (New York: Harper & Bros.; 1880), p. v.

phasis. The Commission's Annual Report for 1890–91 explicitly proclaimed the primacy of the motif, in a passage generally attributed to Roosevelt:

> While one of the main purposes of the law is to improve the public service, yet this can hardly be considered its prime object. Its prime object is to remove from American politics the degrading influences of the patronage system. Certainly, during the last sixty years, no other one cause has been so potent in tending to degrade American politics. The men who are in office only for what they can make out of it are thoroughly unwholesome citizens, and their activity in politics is simply noxious. . . . The whole patronage system is inimical to American institutions; it forms one of the gravest problems with which Democratic and Republican government has to grapple.[7]

The drive to purge American politics, eliminate waste, tighten administration and protect the subordinate civil service against unbridled patronage preoccupied the champions of reform. They invested little effort in a quest for ways to find men qualified to govern and to draw such men into service. They scarcely even sensed the special requirements of the higher levels of administration, where the execution of policy and the design of machinery mix with the shaping of policy. They took for granted that qualified men would appear as a by-product of the programs on which they concentrated their advo-

[7] Annual Report of the U.S. Civil Service Commission (1890–91), p. 13.

cacy, and regarded the upper levels of civil administration as merely an extension of the lower. Sensitive
though they were to the ways of the spoils system, they
forgot the gap between the need and the demand for
skilled personnel in the civil administration, succumbing
to an illusion that it is in the nature of a government to
want talent in the same measure in which it needs talent.
They lost sight of the positive endeavor required to
stimulate a demand for able civil servants to match the
need; and they also overlooked the less subtle difficulty of
attracting suitable men to fill an enlarged demand. It was
their postulate, sometimes conscious, more often unconscious, that the removal of obstacles would suffice to
generate the demand and induce the supply, and that an
invigoration of the subordinate civil service would automatically energize the higher ranks. Let the pathway to
appointive office be cleared of the weeds of patronage; let
subordinate officials be shielded against the sword of
arbitrary removal dangling over their heads; and the road
to government service at all levels would be thronged by
qualified aspirants. So they appeared to assume.

Their propensity was exemplified in Dorman B. Eaton's
study of the Civil Service in Great Britain. In 1877, at the
direction of President Hayes, the Secretary of State
requested Eaton "to investigate and make a report to [the
President] concerning the action of the English government in relation to its Civil Service and the effects of
such action." After two years of study, Eaton published
his report. The final chapter, entitled "A Summary and
the Significance of the Reform Movement," pulled to-

150

gether the author's conclusions concerning the "abuses and reforms" in British administration "and their bearing upon American politics." Only after fifty-eight pages devoted to the principles of the new system of civil service in Great Britain and its practical effects did a reference appear to

One other effect of the merit system [that] is too important not to be noticed—the indirect effect of bringing able and self-reliant young men and women . . . into the departments and local offices. They would soon create an atmosphere of intelligence, thoughtfulness, and independence, which . . . would make it very difficult to treat such offices as the asylums, or the citadels of partisan politics. . . . With better and abler men in the subordinate places, mere politicians—mere strangers to its business, of any sort—would have a hard time indeed, when foisted over such subordinates to the head of a great office. They would be contemptible even in their own estimation. The bare fact that there were many able men in the lower grades would make it certain that the higher places would soon be filled from the lower.[8]

Was it a sunburst of enthusiasm that blinded the reformers to the requirement for a positive program to man a civil service even when organized on a basis of merit? The lapse is hard to understand. It is no less difficult to explain their apparent disregard of the critical distinction between the subordinate levels of a civil

[8] Eaton: *Civil Service in Great Britain,* pp. 400–1.

service and the higher level where administration merges into policy. In the pursuit of their ideal, the reform leaders again and again proved themselves clear-eyed and realistic men. They were aware of the British and presumably not unaware of the Prussian-German experience of civil administration. In opening the battle for reform in 1867, Congressman Thomas Allen Jenckes and his Joint Select Committee on Retrenchment were armed with data and argument derived from correspondence with Stafford A. Northcote and Charles E. Trevelyan, authors of the landmark General Report of 1853 on The Organization of the Civil Service in Great Britain. In 1880, Eaton's *Civil Service in Great Britain* amplified the American knowledge and brought it up to date. Carl Schurz, whose direction of the Department of the Interior under President Hayes was proclaimed a model for all Cabinet officers by the reform leaders, had come to America from his native Germany in the flood of emigration following the collapse of the Revolution of 1848. Immersed in politics in Germany and in civil service reform in the United States, he must have been at least generally aware of the structure and performance of the Prussian civil service. Why then was the status of the Administrative Class in the British Civil Service, the Senior Branch in the British Foreign Service, and the Higher Civil Service of Prussia-Germany so little reflected in the campaigns to reconstitute the American civil administration? If the sagacity of the reform leaders alerted them to the hazards of grafting a British or German twig onto a branch of the American tree, why did they not at least try to identify the potentialities and adapt them to the processes of American life?

Perhaps they believed they had proposed just such an adaptation in a distinction which they emphasized between "political" and "administrative" responsibilities. Aware of the relationship of the Administrative Class and Senior Branch to the class structure of Britain and of the Higher Civil Service to the stratified society of Prussia, they may have regarded a classification of governmental posts into "political" and "administrative" as the nearest to a workable equivalent that could be designed in the fluid American democracy. Perhaps they simply missed the point. At any rate, in their effort to draw a line between "political" and "administrative" offices, they confused two meanings of "political." They blurred the concept of "political" in the sense of identification with a political party into the concept of "political" in the sense of an involvement with policy. Shifting without awareness to and fro between the two usages, they often unconsciously changed the subject while maintaining the language.

Eaton fell victim to the ambiguity in his appraisal of the British Administrative Class.

It is unquestionably essential . . . that a few of the higher executive officers at the head of affairs, who are to carry into effect the policy, both domestic and foreign, of the dominant party, should share the opinions of that party and have faith in its policy. Such higher officers guide all executive affairs, give instructions to all below them, and enforce official obedience everywhere. (In British administration there are from thirty-four to fifty of these higher officers, who are regarded as political, and who go out when their party suffers defeat.) The political opinions of the vast body of subordinate officials, including the whole clerical force, in a properly regulated civil service are not material to the success of such policy. . . ." [9]

Even so penetrating an observer as the young Woodrow Wilson, analyzing congressional government in 1885, confused political responsibility in the party sense with responsibility for policy.

One of the conditions precedent to any real and lasting reform of the civil service, in a country whose public service is moulded by the conditions of self government, is the drawing of a sharp line of distinction between those offices which are *political* and those which are *non-political*. The strictest rules of business discipline, of merit tenure . . . must rule every office whose incumbent has naught to do with *choosing between policies;* but no rules except *the choice of parties* can or should make and unmake, reward or punish, those officers whose privilege it is to fix upon the *political purposes* which administration shall be made to serve. These latter are not many under any form of government. There are said to be but fifty such at most in the civil service of Great Britain; but these

[9] Eaton: *Civil Service in Great Britain*, p. 80. The sentence in parentheses appears in footnote 2 on the same page.

fifty go in or out *as the balance of power shifts from party to party.* In the case of our own civil service it would . . . be extremely hard to determine where the line should be drawn. . . . A doubt exists *as to the Cabinet itself.* Are the Secretaries political or non-political officers?"[1] [Italics added.]

The confusion of meanings obscured the origin of the line between "political" and "administrative." It began as a line of battle between reformers eager to extend and politicians anxious to confine the reach of the Civil Service Act of 1883. To the simplistic crusaders among the reformers and to the machine bosses and heelers among the politicians, the issue was single and precise, and the single purpose was to push the line as far in the chosen direction as they could. In 1890–91, the Civil Service Commission strove to foresee an eventual expansion of the classified civil service upward into the highest sphere of executive responsibility. It regarded most government posts as "purely administrative business offices" and only a very few as "really political in character, after we pass below the highest, such as the members of the Cabinet and the ministers to foreign countries."[2] But a commissioner of the Land Office contemplated any such prospect with a jaundiced eye, candidly avowing his conviction that the classified civil service suited none but minor folk. The line must be drawn, he protested, below chiefs of divisions and chief clerks, who must be ex-

[1] Woodrow Wilson: *Congressional Government,* Ch. V.
[2] Annual Report of the Civil Service Commission (1890–91), p. 15.

cluded because "their relations are not only confidential to the Bureau head but they constitute the last line of demarkation [sic] between the political relations of the Administration and the justly clerical or civil service divisions of the Departments." [3]

There were others—active politicians in sympathy with civil service reform and reform leaders experienced in the operating requirements of government—whose insight denied them either the thrill of the simplistic reformers' vision or the pleasure of the machine politician in feeding the raw appetite for power. Although unable to sort out all the tangled components, they felt in their bones that more was involved than a head-on collision between neatly defined and internally consistent opposing purposes. They sensed the bearing, even if they could not trace the ramifications, of the problem of accommodation between the exigencies of political power and the requirements for the conduct of government. They groped for a more comprehensive and comprehending formulation of the issues and a more varied and sophisticated range of choices. The accomplishment lay beyond their reach, and it was left for later generations.

In their own generation, the champions of civil service reform of the 1870's and 1880's saw the ghost of Andrew Jackson looming up behind their opponents. In their

[3] From a letter of Binger Hermann, Commissioner of the Land Office, in Testimony before a Subcommittee of the Senate Committee on Civil Service and Retrenchment (Govt. Printing Office, 1898), pp. 100–1, published together with S. Rep. 659, 55th Cong., 2d Sess. (1898).

eyes, the presidency of Jackson marked the beginning of degradation in the public service, and threatened their cause as a model followed as cheerfully by Republicans as by Democrats. To undermine its force as a precedent, they invoked earlier precedents. Stigmatizing the Jacksonian doctrine of personnel as a betrayal of the national heritage, they summoned the authority of Washington and the Federalists and Jefferson and the Jeffersonians to redress the alleged distortion.

When President Hayes, in a letter accepting the Republican nomination for president in 1876 and again in his inaugural address in 1877, pledged his incoming administration to civil service reform, he proclaimed his resolve not merely to cleanse the government of "certain abuses and practices of so-called official patronage" but to return "to the principles and practices of the founders of the Government" who "neither expected nor desired from public officers any partisan service. They meant that public officers should owe their whole service to the Government and the people. They meant that the officer should be secure in his tenure as long as his personal character remained untarnished and the performance of his duties satisfactory." [4]

[4] James D. Richardson, *Messages and Papers of the Presidents* (Washington, D.C.: Govt. Printing Office; 1898), VII, 442, 444; see also *Letters and Messages of Rutherford B. Hayes* (Washington, 1881), p. 6.

2

THE FOUNDING FATHERS

There was more to the invocation of the Founding Fathers than platitudes to embellish a proposal for change by presenting it as a return to the true American self. President Hayes called up the facts of a performance that shines in history despite a tarnish of subsequent cant and some blemishes of its own. In Chapter I, in noting the discrepancies between the attributes necessary to win and hold political power and the attributes required to govern, I observed that some men, a few, were amply endowed with both. The United States of America at its birth was blessed with a concentration of such men. The lawyers and merchants of New England and New York and the planters of Virginia made a revolution, seized power, and governed in the full sense. In the main, the men who organized and led the seizure of power in the American Revolution were also the men who organized and directed the new government. Proclaiming it to be the function of governments to vindicate the unalienable rights of men and to establish justice, insure domestic tranquillity, promote the general welfare, and secure the blessings of liberty to the governed, they illuminated the distinction between the bare acquisition and retention of political power and the conduct of government. From Washington's first term as President through Madison's second, and in some degree through the administration of John Quincy Adams, they constituted in themselves an accommodation between the exigencies of political power and the requirements of government. They represent an historical phenomenon comparable, in the terms of politics and government, to the Athens of Pericles in the terms of philosophy and art. Such phenomena glorify mankind and enrich our appreciation of human possibilities. It is good to keep them in mind and take heart from them. But they are too infrequent to be taken as a basis for normal expectations.

When George Washington began to build a national civil administration where none had existed, he set standards of merit in the selection of men that departed radically from the English and French patterns. As Washington retained a nostalgic regard for the British government from which he had done so much to break away, he might have been expected to look to British administration as a guide for his own. But the eighteenth-century English concept of civil office as a species of property at the disposal of the Crown or the landed families that dominated Parliament, and the jobbery through which claims to office in England were then typically asserted, could have served him only as an inverse prototype. At the time of his assumption of office as President on April 30, 1789, the storm was brewing in France that broke ten weeks later in the thunderclap of the Bastille. However seminal the French Revolution in ideas and attitudes, the revolutionary confusion offered the new American government no better model in administration than the Bourbon disintegration. In Prussia,

Frederick William I and Frederick II had already elaborated the austere criteria and rigorous procedures of training and selection of the Higher Civil Service. Through the genius and industry of Baron von Steuben, Washington had drawn upon the stores of Prussian military organization and method in the dark days of Valley Forge, and had managed to fit the import to the temper and outlook of the American soldier. In the realm of civil government, however, the gulf between the Hohenzollern autocracy and the new republic yawned wider than in the tasks of war. If a civilian counterpart of von Steuben might nevertheless have been able to transplant some features of the Prussian civil service to the American soil, no such counterpart ever appeared.

Washington drew his concept and method of administration from sources within himself and the life about him. When he confided to Edward Rutledge his anticipation "that one of the most difficult and delicate parts of the duty of my Office [as President] will be that which relates to nominations for appointments,"[5] he knew whereof he spoke. He had had his bellyful of manipulations for power and place in the Continental Army fourteen years earlier. While straining to shape the embryonic army at Cambridge in 1775, he had erupted to Colonel Joseph Reed, his military secretary: "Such a dearth of public spirit, and want of virtue, such stock-jobbing, and fertility in all the low arts to obtain advan-

[5] Letter of May 5, 1789, in *The Writings of George Washington*, ed. John C. Fitzpatrick, George Washington Bicentennial Edition (Washington, D.C.: Govt. Printing Office, 1939), XXX, 308, 309.

tage of one kind or another, in this great change of
military arrangement, I never saw before, and pray God I
may never be witness to it again. What will be the
ultimate end of these manoeuvers is beyond my scan. I
tremble at the prospect . . . and such a dirty, mercenary spirit pervades the whole, that I should not be at all
surprised at any disaster that may happen. . . . Could I
have foreseen what I have, and am likely to experience,
no consideration upon earth should have induced me to
accept this command." [6] Characteristically, he had recov-
ered his composure when he had to lift the spirits of
others. A week after his outburst to Reed, he rallied
Philip Schuyler, dejected from similar causes: "I have
met with Difficulties of the same sort, and such as I never
expected; but they must be borne with. The Cause we are
engaged in is so just and righteous, that we must try to
rise superior to every Obstacle in its Support; . . ." [7]

As John Marshall never forgot "that it is a *constitution*
we are expounding," so Washington always kept in mind
that he and his colleagues were constituting a nation. His
awareness of the potentiality of precedent in every act
colored his assessment of men and measures. Ten days
after his inauguration, he solicited the opinions of John
Adams, John Jay, and Alexander Hamilton "on the
following points: 1st. Whether a line of conduct, equally
distant from an association with all kinds of company on

[6] Ford: *Writings of George Washington* (New York: G. P.
Putnam's Sons, 1889) III, 246–7 (Letter of 28 November
1775).
[7] Letter of December 5, 1775, in George Washington Bicentennial Edition, IV, 147, 148.

the one hand and from a total seclusion from Society on the other, ought to be adopted by [the President]? and, in that case, how is it to be done? . . . Whether it would tend to prompt impertinent applications and involve disagreeable consequences [for the President each morning at eight o'clock] to give Audience to persons who may have business with him? . . . Whether there would be any impropriety in the President's making informal visits; that is to say, in his calling upon his acquaintances or public Characters for the purposes of sociability or civility; . . . Whether, during the recess of Congress, it would not be advantageous to the interests of the Union for the President to make the tour of the United States, in order to become better acquainted with their principal Characters and internal Circumstances, as well as to be more accessible to numbers of well-informed persons, who might give him useful information and advices. . . ." To explain his concern with matters which might appear trivial, Washington added: "Many things which appear of little importance in themselves and at the beginning, may have great and durable consequences from their having been established at the commencement of a new general government." [8]

He chose his Cabinet and subordinate officers with the same perspective, sensitive to the effect of the first few incumbents in shaping the contours of a new office. To Thomas Jefferson, mildly hesitant to leave his post as Minister to France for a proffered nomination as Secre-

[8] George Washington Bicentennial Edition, XXX, 319–21.

tary of State, Washington declared "plainly that I wish not to oppose your inclinations; and that, after you shall have been made a little farther acquainted with the light in which I view the Office of Secretary of State, it must be at your option to determine relative to your acceptance of it, or continuance in your Office abroad. I consider the successful Administration of the general Government as an object of almost infinite consequence to the present and future happiness of the Citizens of the United States. I consider the Office of Secretary for the Department of State as *very* important on many accts: . . . And I know of no person, who, in my judgment, could better execute the Duties of it than yourself." [9] Washington's appointments were governed by "fitness of character" as his major criterion and geographical representation as a subsidiary. He aimed to stabilize the new structure and fasten its components together by binding to his administration men from all the states who were leaders, whether in a national or local sense, and whose standing and abilities were attested by their records of positions held, honors received, and work performed.

Insisting on "fitness of character," he sought it only in men of means and education, gentlemen in the American metamorphosis of the British social concept—proprietors of plantations in Virginia and the Carolinas; the Knickerbocker squirearchy of the Hudson Valley; the merchants and lawyers of Boston, New York City, Philadelphia. He did so with no thought of conferring privileges upon the

[9] Ibid., pp. 509, 510.

appointees, but as an exaction of service from those most able to give it. He did it as a matter of course, in the spirit of a practical man who does what has to be done in a sensible way. Neither qualms nor second thoughts seem to have troubled him in defining the scope of his quest for talent by the limits of a social class. His course in this respect appeared to be confirmed by a general acquiescence. As the Jeffersonian Republicans gradually organized into a vocal opposition, their remonstrances were voiced by leaders drawn mainly from the same class. There were other currents running deep that would in time break through to the surface, but thirty-nine years were to elapse before they would carry the American government into the Jacksonian phase of the American Revolution.

If Washington confined his choices to the federalists among the gentlemen during his first term, they were mainly federalists in the original connotation of proponents and supporters of the federal Constitution of 1787–89 rather than the later partisan sense. The shape of political parties to come could be discerned only dimly in the first few years. There were intimations, as in a memorial of the House of Delegates of Virginia denouncing Hamilton's plan for the assumption of state debts by the new federal government as a measure "to erect and concentrate, and perpetuate a large monied interest . . . which . . . must in the course of human events produce one or another of two evils, the prostration of agriculture at the feet of commerce or a change in the present form of Federal government, fatal to the existence of Ameri-

164

can liberty . . ." [1] and in Hamilton's premonitory outburst: "This is the first symptom of a spirit which must
either be killed or will kill the Constitution of the United
States;" [2] as well as in the presage given John Adams of
the back country's self-assertion by the strictures of
William Maclay.

Educated in the classics and the law, with a pen of
some cultivation though often dipped in acid, the Senator
from Pennsylvania could only by a long stretch be
numbered among the simple farmers and backwoodsmen
who later flocked to Jefferson's banner and came into
their own with Andrew Jackson. Coming to the Senate,
however, in 1789 from a farm near Harrisburg, at the
time little more than a frontier town, Maclay identified
himself with the interests of the Pennsylvania farmers
and shared their outlook and feelings. The personality of
Adams grated upon his own from the opening day. When
the minutes noting the first President's first address to the
first Congress were read, they incorporated a phrase of
Adams's describing the address as "His most gracious
speech." Maclay's hackles rose and he protested: "Mr.
President, we have lately had a hard struggle for our
liberty against kingly authority. . . . everything related

[1] Journal, House of Delegates, General Assembly of Virginia
(1790), p. 141. The memorial culminated a campaign opened
by two resolutions of November 3 and November 4, 1790,
attacking "an act, making provision for the debts of the United
States," sponsored in Congress by Hamilton. Journal, House of
Delegates (1790), pp. 35–36, 38.
[2] Letter from Hamilton to John Jay, Nov. 13, 1790, H. C.
Syrett, ed. *Papers of Alexander Hamilton* (Columbia Univ.
Press, 1963), VII, 149.

to that species of government is odious to the people. The words prefixed to the President's speech are the same that are usually placed before the speech of His Britannic Majesty. I know they will give offence. I consider them as improper. I therefore move that they be struck out, and that it stand simply address or speech, as may be judged most suitable." [3] There were other encounters in the same vein. Trivial enough on the surface, they signaled issues that would in a few years divide the emerging political parties. Maclay's pen danced in recording Adams's concern over a "report which mentioned that the President should be received in the Senate chamber and proceed thence to the House of Representatives to be sworn: . . ." Adams invited the Senate to consider a problem: " 'Gentlemen, I feel great difficulty how to act. I am possessed of two separate powers; the one in *esse* and the other in *posse*. I am Vice-President. In this I am nothing, but I may be everything. But I am president also of the Senate. When the President comes into the Senate, what shall I be? I can not be [president] then. No, gentlemen, I can not, I can not. I wish gentlemen to think what I shall be' . . . he threw himself back in his chair. A solemn silence ensued. God forgive me, for it was involuntary, but the profane muscles of my face were in tune for laughter in spite of my indisposition." [4]

[3] *The Journal of William Maclay* (1789–91), Journal entry of May 1, 1789. Published under title *Sketches of Debate in the First Senate of the United States*, ed. Harris (Harrisburg, Pa., 1880); conveniently available in an edn. publ. by Albert and Charles Boni (New York, 1927).
[4] Ibid., journal entry of April 25, 1789.

In pointing the moral as he saw it, Maclay articulated suspicions that embittered the Jeffersonian Republicans eleven years later in the election of 1800: "that the motives of the actors in the late Revolution were various can not be doubted. . . . the exalted motives of many revolutionists . . . were . . . the amelioration of government and bettering the condition of mankind. . . . Yet there were not wanting a party whose motives were different. They wished for the loaves and fishes of government, and cared for nothing else but a translation of the diadem and scepter from London to Boston, New York, or Philadelphia; or, in other words, the creation of a new monarchy in America, and to form niches for themselves in the temple of royalty." [5]

By the beginning of Washington's second term, two parties had taken form, along lines defined chiefly by attitudes toward the rival policies identified with Alexander Hamilton or Thomas Jefferson. Usage quickly appropriated the designation of Federalist, originally descriptive of the champions of the new Constitution, to the party that rallied to the ideas of Hamilton and the personalities of Washington, Adams, and Hamilton. Under the leadership of Jefferson, the opposition crystallized into a force resisting Hamilton and pursuing affirmative purposes of its own. The lineal ancestors of the Democrats of a later day, derided as "Jacobins" by the more vehement of the Federalists, they styled themselves formally as Republicans.

Distinct by 1792, the party confrontation sharpened in

[5] Ibid., journal entry of May 1, 1789.

the campaign of 1796 culminating in the election of John Adams, and mounted to a peak of intensity during Adams's term of office. In a parallel progression, allegiance to the Federalist Party came to displace loyalty to the Constitution of 1787–9 as a test of eligibility for office. Faithful to the standard set by Washington as well as his own convictions, Adams reined in partisanship to keep it within the bounds of fitness of character and ability, but he sought the fit among the party faithful, not only for the higher offices but in a growing measure for the lesser. Where Washington had confined his selections to the class of gentlemen as a matter of course, Adams did so both as a matter of course and as a matter of principle.

The people, in all nations [he wrote] are naturally divided into two sorts, the gentlemen and the simplemen, a word which is here chosen to signify the common people. By gentlemen are not meant the rich or the poor, the high-born or the low-born, the industrious or the idle; but all these who have received a liberal education, an ordinary degree of erudition in liberal arts and sciences, whether by birth they be descended from magistrates and officers of government, or from husbandmen, merchants, mechanics, or laborers; or whether they be rich or poor. We must, nevertheless, remember, that *generally* those who are rich, and descended from families in public life, will have the best education in arts and sciences, and therefore the gentlemen will ordinarily, notwithstanding some exceptions to the rule, be the richer, and born

168

of more noted families. By the common people we mean laborers, husbandmen, mechanics, and merchants in general, who pursue their occupations and industry without any knowledge in liberal arts or sciences, or in any thing but their own trades or pursuits; though there may be exceptions to this rule, and individuals may be found in each of these classes who may really be gentlemen.[6]

A Senator Maclay might have loaded his gun with Adams's words and fired charges of Federalist yearning for the fleshpots of monarchy. His shots might have struck home in some Federalist quarters. In Adams's case, he would have missed the point, revealed by the context from which the passage has too often been wrenched. Adams was expounding the bases of his belief in a constitution of checks and balances. In his view, no other foundation could support a realistic hope for men to govern in freedom and justice. It would be folly to ignore the ubiquitous manifestations of original sin. The few who were favored by skill and fortune would tend to aggrandize their lot at the expense of the many. "There is a constant energy and effort in the minds of the [few] to increase the advantages they possess over the [common people], and to augment their wealth and influence at their expense."[7] The many would tend to vent their resentment in a quest for a protector and so raise up a

---

[6] "A Defense of the Constitutions of Government of the United States of America," in *The Works of John Adams* (Boston: Little, Brown; 1851), VI, 185.
[7] Ibid.

Caesar. "The common people, against the gentlemen, established a simple monarchy in Caesar at Rome, in the Medici at Florence, etc., and are now in danger of doing the same thing in Holland. . . ." [8] The class of gentlemen by its very nature, as conceived by Adams, must be open at all times to new entrants, and the membership must be constantly enlarged through universal education at the public expense. "If nations should ever be wise, instead of erecting thousands of useless offices, or engaging in unmeaning wars, they will make a fundamental maxim of this, that no human being shall grow up in ignorance." [9] But it would be vain to hope for public sagacity and virtue alone to curb the primordial tendencies of men. They must be controlled through an institutional distribution and balance of political power. Within such a framework, the talents of the able and the knowledge of the educated may be safely sought out and put to use; and the educated and talented must be preferred in appointments for the effective conduct of the government.

The leader of the opposition did not miss the point. In the circumstances of 1796, Thomas Jefferson, biding his time for the victory soon to come, saw in Adams a bulwark against machinations by the Hamilton faction that dominated the Federalist Party. Jefferson had his own view of the need for an aristocracy and its true nature. He preferred to speak of "*aristoi*," to emphasize the original meaning. He distinguished the "*aristoi*," a natural aristocracy grounded in virtue and talent, from

[8] Ibid., p. 186.   [9] Ibid., p. 168.

the "pseudo-*aristoi*," an artificial aristocracy of wealth
and birth. In a famous letter to Adams, he measured his
concept of aristocracy against the other, noting the areas
of overlap and departure. Like Adams, he proclaimed the
wisdom of appointing only the able and well-educated to
government offices, stipulating that they must be sought
and found among the "natural *aristoi*." While he joined
in Adams's insistence upon constitutional checks against
political domination by the aristocracy of wealth and
birth, he deplored reverse checks against the many. He
rejected Adams's distrust of the old Adam in the people,
summoning a record of thirty years in fifteen or twenty
colonial legislatures in an effort to prove that property
and wealth needed no special institutional protection
against popular majorities.

While Adams would presumably have snorted at so
untroubled a faith in popular virtue, he would not have
hesitated to accept talent and virtue as the touchstones of
the true gentleman. He had made his position plain in his
Defense of the Constitutions of Government of the
United States of America, adding his conviction that the
qualities would be found more often among the liberally
educated than elsewhere and that the liberally educated
would usually be the wealthy and the well-born. However
Jefferson may have appraised the statistical validity of
the Adams estimate of probabilities, he spurned it as a
philosophical basis for political conduct. In effect, however, he adopted it in practice during his tenure of the
presidency after his triumph in the elections of 1800. He
repaired to the standard of merit in appointments raised

by Washington, as Adams had done, and, like Adams, maintained it in essence though with somewhat less consistency and distinction than the first President. Like Washington and Adams, he appointed chiefly men of property and position. While continuing the pattern of merit and gentlemen, he broke from it in choosing Republicans rather than Federalists from among the gentlemen of merit.

Jefferson introduced an additional factor of partisanship in appointments that bore an omen for the future. Washington in the later phases of his presidency and Adams throughout his term had confined appointments to the Federalists, but rarely if ever had they removed incumbents because of party affiliation. Questions of removal would hardly have arisen for them, since they had received no inheritance of appointments from the opposite party. Jefferson extended the criterion of party attachment from appointments to an occasional removal from office. Lamenting the practice as a necessity imposed upon him, he took pains to fix the blame on his predecessors. In a reply to a remonstrance from merchants of New Haven against the removal of one Goodrich, he reminded his correspondents of the virtual monopoly of all offices in the national government by Federalists that confronted him upon his inauguration. In simple duty, how could he tolerate the persistence of a monopoly by a minority who had been repudiated by the American people at the polls? A "due participation of office" by the majority was "a matter of right" and not merely of power. "It would have been to me a circumstance of great relief, had I found a moderate participation of office in the hands of the majority. I would gladly have left to time and accident to raise them to their just share. But their total exclusion calls for prompter corrections. I shall correct the procedure; but that done, . . . shall return with joy to that state of things, when the only questions concerning a candidate shall be, Is he honest? Is he capable? Is he faithful to the Constitution?" [1] He would proceed in the "painful office" with deliberation, "that it may injure the best men least, and effect the purposes of justice and public utility with the least private distress."

From the record, it does not appear that events permitted Jefferson the politician to "return with joy to that state of things" for which Jefferson the philosopher longed. But the problem of removals diminished steadily through a succession of Republican victories, in the reelection of Jefferson in 1804 and the election and reelection of Madison in 1808 and 1812. Sinking under the impact, the Federalist Party expired by its own hand in the odium following the Hartford Convention of 1814, in which Federalists from Massachusetts, Connecticut, and Rhode Island flirted in secret session with a proposal of the Essex Junto that skirted along the edge of secession from the Union and a separate peace with Great Britain in the War of 1812. The election of 1816 was the last in which the Federalist Party put a candidate into the field, to be snowed under by Monroe.

Two Republicans contested the issue in 1820, with the

[1] From a letter to Elias Shipman and others, a committee of the merchants of New Haven, July 12, 1801, in *Works of Thomas Jefferson*, ed. P. L. Ford (New York: G. P. Putnam's Sons, 1905), IX, 270, 274.

Republican Monroe emerging victorious over the Republican John Quincy Adams. When by grace of the preference of the House of Representatives, Adams defeated Jackson and succeeded Monroe in 1824, he ran as the candidate of a Nationalist wing of the Republican Party against the surge of a Democratic wing of the same party behind Andrew Jackson. In the anguished view of his family, after John Quincy Adams came the deluge, and the perspective of almost a century did not alter their judgment. Ninety years after the torrent of Jacksonian democracy inundated John Quincy Adams in the election of 1828, his grandson spoke for him: "When the constitution had been adopted and the first administration organized, General Washington's personality had been so commanding that he had raised, as it were, the whole nation to his own level, by a sort of miracle of inherent strength; but after General Washington died, the democratic system of averages began its work, and the old inequality sank to a common level. By 1828, a level of degradation had been reached, and it was the level of Jackson." [2]

3

ANDREW JACKSON

The pen was the pen of Brooks Adams, but the political premises were the premises of John. Brooks's assessment

[2] Brooks Adams, "The Heritage of Henry Adams," published as an introduction to Henry Adams: *The Degradation of the Democratic Dogma* (New York: The Macmillan Company; 1919), p. 84.

of Jackson reflected his opinion of a democracy inadequately checked and balanced, in the Adams view of adequacy. It contained a kernel of fact which, extracted from the shell of opprobrium, would have been cheerfully acknowledged by the Jacksonians. Andrew Jackson had been carried into the presidency by currents that had washed away much of the former inequality in suffrage. The "democratic system of averages" had begun its work upon the franchise before the death of George Washington. In 1792, Vermont had entered the Union with a constitution that imposed no property qualifications upon the right to vote. Even earlier, in 1776, Pennsylvania, the home of William Maclay, had set taxpaying requirements low enough to enfranchise many farmers and mechanics. The movement broadened steadily. New Jersey abolished both property and taxpaying qualifications in 1807 and Maryland in 1810. The pace quickened with the admission of new states carved out of territories beyond the Alleghenies. Indiana, entering the Union in 1816, Illinois in 1818, and Alabama in 1819 extended the suffrage to all white males, as did Maine, admitted in 1820. The restrictions in the older states bent under the pressure. Connecticut in 1818 and Massachusetts and New York in 1821 abolished or reduced property qualifications. The resistance dug in its heels and prophesied doom as it yielded. The debates in the Constitutional Convention of New York in 1821 exemplified the style of the conflict.

When Thomas Jefferson carried New York in 1804, Madison in 1808, and Monroe in 1816, the state exercised its choice through electors named by its legislature.

Barely 6 per cent of the population could qualify to vote for governor, lieutenant governor, or members of the state senate, through proof of ownership of real estate valued at not less than $250; perhaps 18 per cent, through property ownership of $50 or more, could qualify to vote for members of the state assembly. When the population quadrupled from 340,120 in 1790 to 1,372,812 in 1820, the increment, chiefly small farmers and farm hands in the northern and western counties and factory labor in the cities, clamored for the vote. The Democratic Republicans, dominant in the legislature in 1820, gave heed and pushed through a bill for a constitutional convention. They were checked by the Council of Revision, made up of the governor (George Clinton), the Chancellor (Kent), and the judges of the Supreme Court, installed under the existing constitutional scheme as an additional bulwark against democratic excesses, reinforcing the restriction of the suffrage and the interposition of the legislature between the voters' preference and the actual selection of presidential electors. Empowered to veto legislation, the Council exercised its power. Governor Clinton joined in the veto as a gambit in a game of his owned played against Van Buren for stakes within the Democratic Republican Party, while Chancellor Kent, Chief Justice Ambrose Spencer and their judicial colleagues wielded the veto in vindication of Hamiltonian principles to which they clung.

The Council of Revision did not underestimate the forces surging against it. It sought to maneuver them to its own purposes, purporting to justify its veto as a means to condition a call for a constitutional convention upon the prior sanction of the citizenry. The Democratic Republicans adjusted their tactics in favor of an amended bill submitting a proposal for a constitutional convention to the polls, under a stipulation that all adult white males who paid taxes or had served in the militia must be authorized to participate under a special franchise for the occasion. The Council acquiesced, in silent preparation for the battle to come. The people endorsed the proposal in a flood of votes that portended their choice of delegates and the ultimate outcome. When the New York Constitutional Convention of 1821 assembled, it numbered 110 Democratic Republicans, 13 Federalists and three personal followers of Governor Clinton in its membership.

The Convention's Committee on the Suffrage recommended an article for the proposed new constitution enfranchising every adult male resident who "within the year next preceding the election, paid a tax to the State or county, assessed upon his real or personal property" or was exempted from taxation, or "shall have performed within that year military duty in the militia of this State; or who shall be exempted from performing militia duty in consequence of being a fireman in any city, town, or village," or who "shall have been within the last year, assessed to labor upon the public highways, and shall have performed the labor, or paid an equivalent therefor." [3] To Chancellor Kent, the article amounted to "uni-

[3] Constitution of 1821 of the State of New York, Article Second, Section 1.

versal suffrage," which would be "too mighty an excitement for the moral condition of men to endure. The tendency of universal suffrage is to jeopardize the rights of property and the principles of liberty. There is a constant tendency . . . in the poor to covet and share the plunder of the rich; in the debtor to relax or avoid the obligations of contract; in the majority to tyrannize over the minority, and trample down their rights; in the indolent and profligate to cast the whole burthen of society upon the industrious and virtuous; and there is a tendency in ambitious and wicked men to inflame these combustible materials. . . . Society is an institution for the protection of property as well as life, and the individual who contributes only one cent to the common stock ought not to have the same power and influence in directing the property concerns of the partnership as he who contributes his thousands. He will not have the same inducements to care and diligence and fidelity. . . . We have to apprehend the oppression of minorities, and a disposition to encroach upon private right . . . and to weaken, degrade and overawe the administration of justice. . . . We stand, therefore, on the brink of fate, on the very edge of a precipice." [4] His colleague, Judge Van Ness, reminded the Convention that "by an irreversible decree of Providence, it was pronounced that the poor ye have always with you . . . But what was the

[4] Quoted in *History of the State of New York*, ed. Alexander C. Flick, published under the auspices of The New York State Historical Association (New York: Columbia University Press; 1934), VI, 24.

[5] Ibid., p. 27.

character of the poor? Generally speaking, vice and poverty go hand in hand." [5] General Van Rensselaer, the "last of the patroons," saw the shadow of the Gracchi and agrarian distribution darkening the future of New York; and Abraham Van Vechten of Albany fortified his Federalist brethren with a blunt logic as convincing to himself as it was infuriating to the Democrats: "Life and liberty are common to all, but the possession of property is not. Hence the owners of property have rights which, in relation to those who are destitute, are separate and exclusive." [6]

The spiritual heirs of Hamilton fought a fight which they believed good, but their course was finished. The Convention rolled to its foregone conclusion. The outlook of the majority was typified by the views of two of the Democratic Republican delegates. Radcliffe reminded the Federalists that society was not a commercial company in which the dollar values of shares held determined the votes of the participants but an association of free men for the common good. General Erastus Root added his explanation with a candor as naked as Abraham Van Vechten's. Root emphasized the virtue of enfranchising all who served in the militia: "Not one in ten of these young militiamen would vote for a haughty, proud, domineering aristocrat; they will vote for *republicans*." [7]

The proposed extension of the suffrage was adopted and the Council of Revision was abolished. The end of the Convention did not mark the full reach of the tide. In

[6] Ibid., p. 25.   [7] Ibid., p. 28.

179

an amendment of 1826, the residual restrictions upon white male suffrage were eliminated; the choice of presidential electors was transferred from the legislature to the voting public; and justices of the peace, previously appointed by joint action of county boards of supervisors and the judges of county courts or, in the event of disagreement among them, by the governor, were made elective. In 1833 and 1839, the Constitution of New York was again amended to transfer the selection of mayors from the common councils of the several cities to the populace. A final vestige of property qualifications that had been retained in the Constitution of 1821, conditioning eligibility to the offices of governor, lieutenant governor, or state senator upon the ownership of a freehold, was swept out as an anachronism in 1845.

The political process in other states of the Union moved in a comparable rhythm, gradually shifting the basis of apportionment of electoral districts from a count of taxpayers to a census of population, and augmenting the number of public officers chosen by popular elections. In the election of 1828 that elevated Jackson to the White House, all except Delaware and South Carolina among the twenty-four states chose their presidential electors wholly or mainly by popular ballot.

The multiplication of voters and elective offices bred new occasions for party organization, and demanded more organizers and more time to make the organization effective. If professional politicians had not previously been unknown, they had been few and inconspicuous. They increased in numbers and prominence. Sharpening their skills in the cities, counties, and states, they itched for larger spheres and made alliances across state lines. In the first ten presidential elections, the candidates had been nominated by the leaders in Congress grouped, after the rise of parties, in congressional party caucuses. The grip of King Caucus was broken after 1824. Control over nominations passed to the party organizations and professional politicians of the states, working initially through state conventions or legislatures, coming together in 1832 and thereafter in national party conventions.

The currents converged in the presidential election of 1828. The New England states, New Jersey, Delaware, and more than half of Maryland, standing with John Quincy Adams and the National Republicans, could muster only eighty-three electoral votes for Adams. The farmers, mechanics, and laborers of New York, organized through the Democratic Party by Van Buren and the "Albany Regency," swung twenty of New York's thirty-six electoral votes into Andrew Jackson's column. They were augmented by all the electors of Pennsylvania, chosen in a Democratic sweep organized by professional politicians under the leadership of James Buchanan. The farmers and backwoodsmen of the West, rallying behind a man of their own, carried all the states beyond the Alleghenies for Jackson. The Jeffersonian planters of the South, looking down their noses at the border captain, and Southern hunters and farmers, looking up to him with roaring fellowship, swelled the tally for Jackson in the electoral college to 178.

> They follow behind him, the lusty crew
> Of the States with the Injun trophies.
> They'll sweep him into the White House, too,
> And cock their boots on the sofys.[8]

The famous crowds that swarmed into Washington for the inauguration of Jackson, nettling Justice Story into unjudicial pique—"The reign of King 'Mob' seemed triumphant"—came not only to shout their triumph but to vindicate it through jobs in an administration they accounted their own. They stirred feelings in Old Hickory that President Garfield would come to understand in his time. In a reflection upon the experience, Jackson wrote: "It appeared that instead of love of principle it was love of office that had induced [many of] them to support the good cause as they please to term it. . . ."[9]

However natural Andrew Jackson's moods of annoyance or depression, he was hardly an innocent victim of circumstance. He believed in a policy of rotation in office, although by no means in the unbridled measure with which he has often been charged, and his belief rested on grounds broader and deeper than the mere partisan utility of patronage. He expounded his philosophy in his first Annual Message to Congress on December 8, 1829:

> There are, perhaps, few men who can for any great length of time enjoy office and power without being

[8] Rosemary and Stephen Vincent Benet, "Andrew Jackson," in *A Book of Americans* (New York: Farrar and Rinehart; 1933), pp. 60, 61.
[9] Andrew Jackson Papers, in Library of Congress, 2nd Series, Vol. V, Item 242; quoted in Marquis James, *Andrew Jackson* (New York: Garden City Publishing Co.; 1940), p. 490.

more or less under the influence of feelings unfavorable to the faithful discharge of their public duties. Their integrity may be proof against improper considerations immediately addressed to themselves, but they are apt to acquire a habit of looking with indifference upon the public interests and of tolerating conduct from which an unpracticed man would revolt. Office is considered as a species of property, and government rather as a means of promoting individual interests than as an instrument created solely for the service of the people. Corruption in some and in others a preversion of correct feelings and principles divert government from its legitimate ends and make it an engine for the support of the few at the expense of the many. The duties of all public officers are, or at least admit of being made, so plain and simple that men of intelligence may readily qualify themselves for their performance; and I can not but believe that more is lost by the long continuance of men in office than is generally to be gained by their experience. I submit, therefore, to your consideration whether the efficiency of the Government would not be promoted and official industry and integrity better secured by a general extension of the law which limits appointments to four years.

In a country where offices are created solely for the benefit of the people no one man has any more intrinsic right to official station than another. Offices were not established to give support to particular men at the public expense. No individual wrong is, therefore, done by removal, since neither appointment to nor continuance in office is matter of right. The incumbent became an officer with a view to public benefits, and when these require his removal they are not to be sacrificed to private interests. It is the people, and they alone, who have a right to complain when a bad officer is substituted for a good one. He who is removed has the same means of obtaining a living that are enjoyed by the millions who never held office. The proposed limitation would destroy the idea of property now so generally connected with official station, and although individual distress may be sometimes produced, it would, by promoting that rotation which constitutes a leading principle in the republican creed, give healthful action to the system.[1]

The professional politicians who supported Jackson had their own approach to his philosophy of administration and personnel. With little taste for the formulation of such doctrine, they had a lusty appetite for its application, and they applied it in their own fashion. Senator William Learned Marcy of New York spoke their mind in the Senate debate on whether to advise and consent to Jackson's nomination of Van Buren as Minister to Great Britain. When Henry Clay denounced the nominee as the "gentleman [to whom] is principally to be ascribed the introduction of the odious system of pro-

[1] James D. Richardson (ed.), *Messages and Papers of the Presidents* (1896) II, 447, 448–9; also conveniently available in F. N. Thorpe (ed.), *The Statesmanship of Andrew Jackson as Told in His Writings and Speeches* (New York: The Tandy-Thomas Co.; 1909), 44–45.

scription . . . in the Government of the United States
. . . the system on which the party in his own State,
of which he is the reputed head, constantly acts . . . a
detestable system, drawn from the worst periods of the
Roman republic . . . [in which] offices, honors and dig-
nities [would be] put up to a scramble, to be decided by
the result of every Presidential election," [2] Marcy met the
Kentuckian head on:

> It may be, sir, that the politicians of the United States
> are not so fastidious as some gentlemen are, as to
> disclosing the principles on which they act. They
> boldly preach what they practice. When they are
> contending for victory, they avow their intention of
> enjoying the fruits of it. If they are defeated, they
> expect to retire from office. If they are successful, they
> claim, as a matter of right, the advantages of success.
> They see nothing wrong in the rule, that to the victor
> belong the spoils of the enemy.[3]

To the extent that Jackson has been tarred with
Marcy's brush in the contemplation of history, it may
fairly be said that Jackson "asked for it." There was an
overlapping of purposes and, in a larger measure, of
consequences. The mischief wrought or facilitated or at
least made possible by Jackson became the bitter legacy
which the civil service reformers rejected and fought to
replace in the latter half of the nineteenth century. The
Jacksonian phase of the American Revolution eroded the

[2] Gales and Seaton's Register of Debates, 22nd Cong., 1st Sess.,
p. 1324 (January 24–25, 1832).
[3] Ibid., p. 1325.

accommodation between the demands of political power and the needs of effective government that had been established in the Federalist and early Jeffersonian phases. These are verifiable entries in the Jackson reckoning, but they do not complete the account. There were other items, overlooked too often or noted with scant appreciation of their significance.

Instinctively, gropingly, Andrew Jackson located and probed a weakness in the American government of his day. As political power and participation had spread through American society, the center of gravity had shifted. To the new holders of power—the "people . . . the farmer, the mechanic, and the laboring classes of society" [4] to whom Jackson felt bound by a sense of duty and affinity, believing that "to labour for the good of the masses was a special mission assigned to him by his Creator" [5]—the Federalist-Jeffersonian accommodation through the appointment of gentlemen of merit had ceased to be relevant. They regarded it as neither useful for the execution of their purposes nor dependable as an instrument of their power. An accommodation between men qualified to take and hold power and men qualified to govern involves a reciprocal acceptance of the respective roles. The former must adjust their position to the operating requirements of the latter, and the latter must attune their conduct to the position of the former and its

[4] From Andrew Jackson's Farewell Address of March 4, 1837, James D. Richardson, *Messages and Papers of the Presidents*, III, 292, 300.
[5] Van Buren, quoted in Arthur M. Schlesinger, Jr.: *The Age of Jackson* (Boston: Little, Brown & Company; 1945), p. 43.

human implications. To the people newly come to political power, the civil administration inherited from the
Federalist-Jeffersonian accommodation showed little disposition to get in tune. In their view and to an extent in
fact, it tended to frustrate rather than acknowledge their
new position. These are matters of degree, encompassing
endless variations in shading, shifting transitions and
subtleties of interaction always contained in a complex
political relationship. After all allowances duly made, a
residue remained that was real and felt by Jackson's
"people . . . the farmer, the mechanic and the laboring
classes of society." To a degree, they had come to feel
alienated, and the degree was significant. Jacksonian
democracy gave them a sense of identification with their
government that was essential to its vitality and even to
its survival in crises. In a nation imbued with movement
and innovation, Jacksonian democracy refreshed the
public administration with men drawn from the society,
alert to the processes of change. In a society committed
to the view that governments derive their just power
from the consent of the governed and exist to vindicate
the rights of men, the broadened participation of the
people in government through appointive offices as well
as elective carried a moral justification of its own. The
virtues of Jacksonian democracy defined future requirements for the public administration in America more
than its vices. Whatever new accommodations American
instincts and imagination might devise from time to time
between the factors of political power and constructive
government, they would be effective and durable only if

consistent with the American imperatives revealed through Jackson: a popular sense of identification with the public administration and the fact of popular participation in it.

I return to the liabilities in the balance sheet. Through the rotation of offices, carried in time well beyond the limits set by Jackson (estimated by Samuel Eliot Morison and Henry S. Commager at 252 out of 612 presidential appointments and about one in fourteen of the Post Office Department, and by Arthur M. Schlesinger, Jr., as between 10 and 20 per cent of the incumbents), Jacksonian democracy broke down the accommodation inherited from the Founding Fathers. Neither the Jacksonian Democrats, nor the Whigs who evolved from the National Republicans in their turn, made any serious attempt at replacement. They were oblivious to the need, sharing Andrew Jackson's conviction that the "duties of all public officers are . . . so plain and simple that men of intelligence may readily qualify themselves for their performance." In the circumstances of American society and government in the decades between Andrew Jackson and the Civil War, they could avoid or postpone a reckoning, for the requirements of many public offices were comparatively simple, the margin for error in their calculations was wide, and the reserve capacity of the nation to absorb losses was great.

But the days were fast approaching when "A million wheels went round and round,/And we built right up into the sky,/And dug way down into the ground." The Industrial Revolution, which had spread to America and settled in the congenial land, would follow the pioneers along the westward trails and in time establish its new home as its premier show place. In the eighty years following the assassination of President Garfield and the passage of the Pendleton Civil Service Act, the gross national product, adjusted to constant prices, would multiply fourteenfold. The population of the United States would double between 1828 and 1852, double again by 1880, double again by 1914, and virtually double yet again by 1965. American military forces would fight in Europe, Asia, and Africa and patrol the seven seas; American economic resources would pour through the channels of government into scores of other states; and America would take part in regional and worldwide associations of states which it would help to build and to lead.

The belief would become widespread that modern industry and agriculture have the potential capacity to meet the age-old economic anxieties of men, and that government is a major and indispensable instrument for realizing the potential. Theodore Roosevelt's "Square Deal," Woodrow Wilson's "New Freedom," Franklin Roosevelt's "New Deal," Harry Truman's "Fair Deal," John F. Kennedy's "New Frontier," and Lyndon Johnson's "Great Society" would reflect the popular conviction that government must serve as a positive force in the endeavor to achieve economic security and growth and to vindicate the principle of justice throughout American society. With the development of nuclear energy and nuclear weapons and the emergence of the Soviet Union and

Communist China as primary threats to peace, the problems of war and peace, economic security and economic growth under the stresses and opportunities of modern technology, and the preservation and vindication of freedom would overlap and interpenetrate.

The reckoning to which the champions of civil service reform tried to call the Jacksonian administrative tradition in the decades following the Civil War would confront Americans again and again, on terms progressively more demanding. Time and circumstance would renew the relevance of George Washington's conviction that "the successful Administration of the general Government [is] an object of almost infinite consequence to the present and future happiness of the Citizens of the United States" as well as Washington's insistence upon "fitness of character" as a fundamental criterion for appointments to office. In the continuing evolution of their government, Americans would have to redefine "fitness of character" in terms of contemporary requirements but maintain its essence. Insisting on fitness, they would need to stay mindful of the lasting pertinence of the Jacksonian imperatives of popular participation and a popular sense of identification with the public administration in the appointive sector as well as the elective. They would have to learn how to vindicate the successful development of the general government in its administrative aspect no less than its political.

CHAPTER VIII

AN AMERICAN ACCOMMODATION

It is the fashion among dilettanti and fops (perhaps I myself am not guiltless) to decry the whole formulation of the active politics of America, as beyond redemption and to be carefully kept away from. See that you do not fall into this error. . . . Thought you greatness was to ripen for you like a pear?

Walt Whitman, *Democratic Vistas*

1

THE PRESIDENCY AS AN ADMINISTRATIVE INSTITUTION

The presidency has been pre-eminent as a political institution from the start, marking the national government directly by the stamp of strong presidents and inversely through the consequences of the weak. The posture of the presidency as an administrative institution has been another story. Its administrative structure, if structure it could be called, barely emerged before 1857. Remaining rudimentary throughout the nineteenth century and into the twentieth, it became three-dimensional only after the first World War.

In the beginning, no funds were appropriated to the presidency for staff or clerical assistance of any kind. General Washington had enjoyed the secretarial assistance of his military aids. President Washington, denied any such official comfort, had to shift for himself. Relying initially upon the faithful Tobias Lear, his personal secretary who accompanied him to the White House from Mount Vernon, Washington was soon driven to engage the services of his nephews, Robert and Howell Lewis. They labored as copyists paid, like Lear, out of their uncle's personal resources. The family and informal pattern set by Washington persisted as the only arrangement for clerical or administrative assistance available to the first fourteen American presidents, varied on occasion by the nominal employment of a member of the presidential household as a departmental clerk. Not until four years before the Civil War did Congress provide the President with a staff, designated as his "official household," maintained by an aggregate budget of $5,350 a year. The Act of March 3, 1857, enacted on Franklin Pierce's last day in office, allocated $2,500 a year for a private secretary to the President, $1,200 for a steward, $900 for a messenger, and $750 for a contingent fund. Its initial beneficiary, James Buchanan, faithful to the congenial precedent of family preferment, named his nephew as private secretary. From the slight and tardy beginning, sporadic measures added a clerk here, an assistant there, an occasional increment in funds, but little of institutional significance until a national budget system was installed in 1921.

There had always been a budgeting process of a sort in the Executive Branch. Ever since an Act of September 2, 1789, had directed the Secretary of the Treasury to prepare and transmit to Congress estimates of the public revenue and public expenditures, the Secretary had done precisely that, neither more nor less. He had "prepared" his estimates through a mechanical collation of figures drawn up by the departments, and the bureaus within each department, in mutual independence. Neither controlled nor guided by the President nor by any central authority apart from the statutory direction itself, each departmental and bureau chief derived his calculations from the prior year's experience modified by whatever initiatives that might occur to him. As the computations of the bureaus of each department arrived in the departmental head office, they were assembled and passed on to the Treasury, where the staff incorporated them in a "Book of Estimates." Although the Secretary of the Treasury saw to the classification, compilation, indexing, and printing of the Book of Estimates, neither he nor any other executive officer undertook to assess whatever justifications may have been advanced to support the estimates, or to eliminate duplication, harmonize conflicting assumptions, or conform the estimates in the aggregate to a forecast of national needs.

Institutionally, the President had no part in the process. As a practical matter, he could of course exert personal command or influence; but as a practical matter, with only a minimal staff, his capacity to intervene was confined to random or special occasions.

By the Budget and Accounting Act of 1921, Congress inaugurated a national budget system under the direction of the President. A Bureau of the Budget, under a director appointed by the President, was established to operate as a staff instrument of the President under presidential rules and regulations, although located within the Department of the Treasury. The historic implications were exposed by a report of a Select Committee submitting the bill to the House.

To the modern eye, the language of the report is suffused with an air of anachronism. The reader shakes himself and wonders if some typographical mischance might not have substituted a "1921" as the date for an "1821" that should have been there. Pointing out that the existing system "for handling the financial affairs of the government" was grossly defective and that its flaws could "only be adequately met by Congress making definite provision for the establishment of *what is known as a budget system*" (italics added), the Select Committee went on to explain that a "budget system is one under which use is made of *what is known as a budget as the central instrument for determining and making provision for the financial needs* of a government." (Italics added.) With unabated solemnity, the Committee then appraised the "various definitions" which "have been given of the term budget," singling out for approval one to the effect that a budget is "an instrument through which the several financial operations of the Government are collated, compared one with the other, and brought under examination at one and the same time . . . a document

194

through which the chief executive, as the authority responsible for the actual conduct of governmental affairs, comes before the fund-raising and fund-granting authority and makes full report concerning the manner in which he and his subordinates have administered affairs during the last completed year; in which he exhibits the present condition of the Public Treasury, and on the basis of such information sets forth his program of work for the year to come and the manner in which he proposes that such work shall be financed. . . ."

Even after so painstaking an exposition of what today seems evident, the Committee felt moved to continue: "In the National Government there can be no question but that the officer upon whom shall be placed this responsibility is the President of the United States. He is the only officer who is superior to the heads of departments and independent establishments. He is the only officer of the administrative branch who is interested in the Government as a whole rather than in one particular part. He is the only administrative officer who is elected by the people and thus can be held politically responsible for his actions. . . ." [1]

The reader may blink at the implication that the Committee was expounding an abstruse point that would be missed unless hammered home, in the third decade of the twentieth century, in a government which had mobilized a vast economy and directed it through a world war,

[1] Report of The Select Committee on the Budget to Accompany H.R. 30, House Rep. No. 14, 67th Cong., 1st Sess. (April 25, 1921), p. 5.

under a President who had joined the Prime Ministers of Britain, France, and Italy as the "Big Four" to settle the posture of the post-World War I world. The freshman textbook quality of the exposition is today hard to believe. It highlights the disparity in the tempo of development between the political and the administrative aspects of the presidency.

From the turn of the century to the Budget and Accounting Act of 1921, successive Presidents—Theodore Roosevelt, Taft, Wilson—called on their countrymen to consider how the growth of the nation had outrun the structure of the presidency and the Executive Branch. The response signaled by the Budget and Accounting Act of 1921 was not soon renewed. Almost ten years later, President Hoover again invoked the concern of his people for the need to transform the concept and organization of the presidency in its administrative aspect. President Franklin Roosevelt returned to the theme, proclaiming as his twentieth-century predecessors had done before him that the time had come and passed to put the government's house in order, lest self-government break down under the battering of the twentieth century. Following the Reorganization Act of 1939, change came with a rush, accelerating through World War II and its aftermath and persisting through the administrations of Presidents Truman, Eisenhower, Kennedy, and Johnson.

Even if one restricts the frame of reference tightly to the modern period, measuring time relationships by the life span of the United States of America and regarding

2

the American Revolution, the French Revolution, and the onset of the Industrial Revolution as remote beginnings in days of old, one is startled to note how much of the bulk and sinew of the Executive Branch is new. Take up a copy of the *Congressional Directory* and turn to the section on the Executive. The President is listed first, of course, along with his military, naval, and air force aides. Then comes the "Executive Office of the President," created in 1939, an extensible framework containing an assortment of entities. Run your eye down the roster: the White House Office; Bureau of the Budget; Council of Economic Advisers; National Security Council; Central Intelligence Agency; National Aeronautics and Space Council; Office of Emergency Planning; Office of Science and Technology; Office of the Special Representative for Trade Negotiation. They serve the President as professional or clerical staff, or as advisers or representatives in functions involving several departments.

The staff of the White House Office may be considered in part an expansion of the "official household" timorously initiated in 1857. In larger part, it represents an innovation stemming from a President's Committee on Administrative Management of Franklin Roosevelt's day. It took its formal origin and name in an Act of June 25, 1948. Of the Bureau of the Budget, little more need be said. Its formal posture was adjusted to conform to the substance of its operations by its transfer to the Executive Office of the President in 1939; and its duties were augmented to include advice to the President on the organization and management of the executive branch.

The Council of Economic Advisers was created by the Employment Act of 1946; the National Security Council and the Central Intelligence Agency by the National Security Act of 1947; and the National Aeronautics and Space Council by the National Aeronautics and Space Act of 1958. The Office of Emergency Planning, built upon elements originating in World War II, was established in 1958; and the Office of Science and Technology and the Office of the Special Representative for Trade Negotiations in 1962. In short, the administrative establishment of the presidency has emerged mainly since the 1920's and largely since 1939. Its development typifies both the pace and the pattern of growth throughout the Executive Branch in the present century.

2

THE GROWTH OF THE EXECUTIVE BRANCH

As the industrial and scientific revolutions gathered momentum in the United States through the decades spanning the turn from the nineteenth into the twentieth century, the lawyer and the investment banker kept pace with the engineer, constructing the modern corporation as the engineer built the modern assembly line. The rush of production and scale of enterprise generated elation and anxiety. Exulting in the machinery and energy of the age, the populace also feared that none "but those who stood at the levers of control . . . [could] have a chance to look out for themselves." [2] As the exultation was qualified by anxiety, so the anxiety was gentled by a new hope. Americans came to regard the energy and machinery as sources of a potential abundance adequate to end the primordial human fear of want. Casting about for means to exploit the sources, they fastened upon the national government. Theodore Roosevelt and Woodrow Wilson, perceiving the pain and the promise of the new technology from the outlook of leadership, understood the popular fear and hope. They summoned their countrymen to political action through the national government to realize the purposes of American life in the conditions of change. Their call was renewed by six of the eight presidents following Wilson, in their own time and own way—with gusto by Franklin Roosevelt, Harry Truman, John F. Kennedy, and Lyndon Johnson; with misgivings by Herbert Hoover, under the shock of the financial collapse of 1929 and the economic depression; and almost despite himself by Dwight Eisenhower, sympathetic to specific needs notwithstanding his general antipathy to expanding the sphere of the national government. "Today," President Eisenhower reported to Congress in 1956, "we believe as strongly in economic progress through free and competitive enterprise as our fathers did, and we resent as they did any unnecessary intrusion of Government into private afairs. But . . . our agricultural policy . . . [including] the nine-point

[2] Woodrow Wilson: First Inaugural Address, March 4, 1913, in *Supplement to Messages and Papers of the Presidents, Wilson 1913–17* (Washington: Bureau of National Literature; 1917), pp. 7868, 7869.

program built around the Soil Bank put forward in the recent Message on Agriculture . . . [constitutes] a many-sided attack on the ills that beset agriculture. . . . The Government can do a great deal to help people who have been left behind in the onrush of progress by undertaking special programs for raising their productivity. . . . The Rural Development Program is a soundly conceived approach. . . . To cope with chronic unemployment which has persisted in some communities, . . . a new Area Assistance Program is recommended.

"Vocational rehabilitation, widened coverage of the Federal Old-Age and Survivors Insurance Program, and housing needs of older people are fields in which advances should be made. . . . The pooling of risks by private carriers, or if need be through a Federal program, would help meet this problem [of insurance against catastrophic illness]." [3]

A popular demand for economic opportunity and social justice, coupled with a popular will to seek them in part through governmental action, has emerged as the salient domestic political fact of our time. It has drawn other facts in its train. In a quest for economic security and fair shares, the need to increase production can be overlooked. In a drive to control the modern economy through action by the central government, the importance of flexibility and the creative individual mind can be neglected. In pressure toward social justice, it is not

[3] Letter of Transmittal of the Economic Report of the President, January 24, 1956, pp. iii–v.

inconceivable that individual justice can be jeopardized. Events in other lands attest the reality of the hazards. In a preoccupation with the means through government to meet the new demands, it is possible to lose sight of the wisdom distilled from the American experience: the spiritual worth and practical importance of personal freedom and private action, as well as the political and legal institutions that have constituted their historic setting. It is hard to maintain a balance among purposes deeply felt which seem to conflict and in the short run may conflict in fact. It is especially hard when the opinions of millions of vigorous men and women are thrown into the reckoning. Yet, appraised in the long perspective of human error and with due allowance for the innate untidiness of political life, the American people in the first half of the twentieth century have managed to maintain a workable equilibrium. Despite heavy liabilities in the account, on net balance they have gone forward with the job of adjusting their society to the conditions of the age while preserving the heritage of the independent human spirit and the self-reliant mind. Apart from the issues of war and peace, it has been the central political task of Americans in this century to meet the new demands while adjusting them to the old wisdom.

The undertaking has spawned new bureaus and agencies and modified old ones. As a sample from a profusion of possible illustrations, I mention the Department of Health, Education and Welfare and the Social Security Administration within the Department; the National

201

Labor Relations Board; the Securities and Exchange Commission; the Federal Deposit Insurance Corporation; the Federal Communications Commission; the Department of Housing and Urban Affairs; the Small Business Administration; the Wage and Hour Division of the Department of Labor; the Area Redevelopment Administration of the Department of Commerce; the Agricultural Stabilization and Conservation Service and the Rural Electrification Administration of the Department of Agriculture; and the Tennessee Valley Authority. All have come into being or have taken their present character and style since the 1930's, in an acceleration of a trend interrupted by the administrations of Harding and Coolidge but evidenced earlier in Theodore Roosevelt's "Square Deal" and "New Nationalism" and Woodrow Wilson's "New Freedom."

From his inauguration on March 4, 1913, Wilson had seventeen months in which to pursue his domestic goals free from external distraction. Following the outbreak of World War I at the end of July, 1914, the unready republic and its unready President were compelled to turn by degrees from their internal preoccupations to the "incredible European catastrophe." For Wilson, a shadow of unreality brooded over events. For a while, he could even persuade himself that "So far as we are concerned, there is no cause for excitement." But by the spring of 1917, the President with a passion for peace was calling for "Force, Force to the utmost, Force without stint or limit." When the war ended, Wilson did not turn again to the unfinished work of the "New Freedom." He concentrated the residual energies of his fatigue and illness upon a plan for a League of Nations to maintain the peace. His countrymen declined to follow him, in the short run. In a longer view, his insistence that the United States lead in seeking to institute an order of law and peace throughout the world was accepted by the American government and people.

For the past quarter of a century, government in the United States has been dominated by the themes that absorbed Woodrow Wilson. Resistance against aggression and an endeavor to establish a peaceful and productive international order have shaped the foreign aspect. Like the main internal themes—the effort to vindicate human personality while meeting the stresses and realizing the opportunities of modern technology and economic organization—the external undertakings have altered old and generated new departments and agencies. In 1924, the Rogers Act founded a comprehensive Foreign Service of the United States, reconstituted in 1946. The structure for the conduct of foreign affairs has been further enlarged to incorporate Assistant Secretaries of State for International Organization Affairs and Public Affairs; United States missions to the United Nations, the Organization of American States, the North Atlantic Treaty and the Organization for Economic Cooperation and Development; the Agency for International Development; the United States Information Agency; the United States Arms Control and Disarmament Agency; and the Peace Corps. In 1946, the Atomic Energy Commission was established; and in 1947, a Department of the Air Force was founded, the Department of War was converted into a department of the Army, and both departments along with the Department of the Navy were linked together within a newly created Department of Defense.

3

WHITHER SPOILERS? WHITHER REFORMERS?

The jobs confronting the American government today, the complexity of its tools and the cost of blunders would jolt an Andrew Jackson from his belief that the "duties of all public offcers are . . . so plain and simple that men of intelligence may readily qualify themselves for their performance." While Senator William Marcy has heirs of his spirit in contemporary American politics, few on the national scene—if more perhaps in local government— would question the necessity of tempering the spoils of political victory to the requirements of effective government.

In the practice of the Civil Service, much remains of the old preoccupation with protection against patronage at the subordinate levels. But as "civil service reform" broadened into the advancement of public administration, leaders have come to stress the higher levels of administration and positive recruitment throughout. The President's Committee on Administrative Management in 1937 exemplified the new emphasis.

After more than fifty years of experience with civil service in Federal, State, and local governments, there

204

is overwhelming evidence to show that the original theory of merely protecting appointments from political influence through a legalistic system of civil-service administration is inadequate to serve democratic government under modern conditions. There is still need for protection, but the urgent new need today is for the development of a real career service through positive, constructive, modern personnel administration . . . Democratic government today, with its greatly increased activities and responsibilities, requires personnel of the highest order—competent, highly trained, loyal, skilled in their duties by reason of long experience and assured of continuity. . . .[4]

In the higher civil posts, administration blends into the making of policy. It may be possible to separate the two in public commentary or scholarly analysis, where the mind abstracts questions of policy from the matrix in which they are embedded and rounds them into a comprehensive formulation. In the actual conduct of government, policy typically can be touched only at particular points. The course of public policy involves a succession of specific decisions on specific problems that arise in infinite variety. As a practical matter, each problem must be met in the first instance by the man in whose sphere of responsibility it makes itself felt. He may seek to meet the problem alone or draw in associates or superiors. He may meet it actively by doing something or passively by

[4] Report of the President's Committee on Administrative Management, January, 1937 (Govt. Printing Office, 1937), pp. 7, 21.

doing nothing. Whether through action or inaction, his response entails a decision. Day by day and week by week, at points without number, specific decisions of this kind occur. Their cumulative effect over the months and years sets critical limits within which the President, Congress, or the heads of departments find themselves confined when issues emerge from the context of daily operations and loom up greatly before us.

To anticipate and channel such a cumulative effect, one must reach and influence the particular decisions. An attempt to do so case by case would choke the government in a snarl of restraints and bottleneck all decisions in the President's office. It can be done only through the judgment exercised in choosing the men who meet the problems in the first instance. Formulations of policy abstracted from application can have little or no real meaning, and the essential ingredient in application consists of the men through whom the policies are applied. The processes determining the personnel through whom data and issues reach the President or heads of departments and by whom verbal formulations of policy are translated into action largely determine the content of policy. It must be built into the concept and feel of the President's or a Cabinet officer's job that the planning, recruitment, development and utilization of the personnel through whom he does his job are a primary responsibility of his own. He may not relegate the core of the responsibility to specialized administrative or personnel officers, however indispensable such officers may be in organizing the mechanics and facilitating his decisions.

POLICY, POLITICS, AND ADMINISTRATION

Our insights into the choices affecting personnel have gained in sophistication. But we remain bedeviled by old and stubborn sources of confusion. The civil service reformers of the 1880's were by no means the last among their countrymen to be perplexed by the relationships between policy and administration, politics and administration, and policy and politics. The distinction between "political" in relation to a political party and "political" in relation to policy ought to be clear. In the abstract, it appears to be. In application, it continues to elude politicians, administrators, and critics.

It tripped the President's Committee on Administrative Management in 1937. Proclaiming a "need for attracting, retaining, and developing human capacity in the public service," the Committee called for an extension of the "merit system . . . upward, outward and downward to include all positions in the Executive Branch of the Government *except those which are policy-determining in character* [italics added]." [5] If taken literally, the Committee would seem to expect merit to be ignored in appointments to policy-determining positions. Since such an interpretation would contradict their intent, we are left to unravel the reverse tangle of words and meaning. I suggest that two concealed jokers made the mischief. One confused "policy-determining positions" with a few

[5] Ibid.

posts at the top of the executive branch considered properly "political" in the party turnover sense. The Committee presumably did want to exclude the latter from the merit system. The other joker fudged an unspoken distinction between a "merit system," as the term is used by technicians in civil service administration, and a general practice of appointments on the basis of merit. In calling for a "merit system" the Committee was not merely advocating a systematic and consistent pattern of selection governed by merit. It aimed more narrowly at a specific arrangement. The President's Committee appropriated the term "merit system" exclusively for a tightly organized corps uniformly selected and advanced through regular steps in a defined hierarchy of grades. The Committee had in mind a system like the United States Civil Service as it had been and more especially as the Committee envisaged it to be, or the Foreign Service of the United States, or the British Civil Service, or the Prussian-German Civil Service. But appointments may be made systematically on merit apart from such a system.

A glance at the federal judiciary will illuminate the point. Federal judges are appointed in principle and largely in practice on the basis of merit. They are drawn from a trained and experienced professional group and hold office under a tenure whose security could well be the envy of civil servants. Did the President's Committee perhaps dismiss the federal judiciary as somehow irrelevant because of an unconscious assumption that the judicial function automatically implied a different style of organization? A look at the integrated organization of the administrative branches of the German Higher Civil Service and the German judiciary could have set the committee right. The terms of an executive agreement of 1930 between the national government and the states of Germany on preparation for the Higher Civil Service revealed the form of integration. Candidates for the Higher Civil Service, whether in the administrative branches or the judiciary, had to complete a study of "jurisprudence" lasting seven semesters, comprising law, political science, economics, history, and penology. During a candidate's probationary service, he underwent practical training in "the conduct of the judiciary, public prosecution, and prison administration" as well as in "the conduct of administrative departments." [6] A successful candidate acquired eligibility for either a judicial post or an administrative position in the Higher Civil Service. Although transfers between judicial and administrative positions were rare, judges remained eligible candidates in principle for the administrative branches of the Higher Civil Service.

Ten years after President Franklin Roosevelt's Committee on Administrative Management rendered its final report, President Truman initiated a Commission on the Organization of the Executive Branch, under the chairmanship of then former President Herbert Hoover. President Eisenhower resumed the inquiry through a second

[6] *Bekanntmachung* of Nov. 20, 1930 (*Reichsministerialblatt*, p. 547), translated in Marx, "Civil Service in Germany", Monograph No. 5 in White et al., *Civil Service Abroad* (New York: McGraw-Hill; 1935), p. 211.

commission of the same name and under the same chairman. A Task Force on Personnel and Civil Service of the second Hoover Commission submitted recommendations in 1955 keyed to a proposed classification of senior appointed personnel into non-career "political executives" and career "senior civil servants." The "political executives" were to be the "necessary expendables who give flexibility to the machinery of Government and who make it possible for the Chief Executive to adapt his management team to changing circumstances." [7] They were to fill all posts whose incumbents made "final decisions in the establishment of governing policies . . . act publicly in advocating new policies and in justifying . . . the basic principles or philosophy which controls their department or agency policies" or performed duties of a "personal and confidential nature." [8] The senior civil servants, on the other hand, would steer "clear of all political activity, preserve their neutrality in matters of politics," avoid "emotional attachment to the policies of any administration" as well as any personal identification with "a political party or its policies" and make "no public or private statements to the press except of a purely factual nature." [9]

Could the Task Force and Commission really have believed what they appear to have said? Are only execu-

[7] Task Force on Personnel and Civil Service of the Commission on Organization of the Executive Branch of the Government, *Report on Personnel and Civil Service* (Feb., 1955), p. 39.

[8] Commission on the Organization of the Executive Branch, *Personnel and Civil Service: A Report to the Congress* (Feb., 1955), pp. 31–32.

[9] Ibid., p. 39, 41.

tives who are political in the party turnover sense supposed to aid in the formulation or defense of public policies? Are senior civil servants supposed to hold themselves aloof from concern over laws and policies of Congress and the President which they are sworn to uphold and execute? Why is "emotional attachment" to a policy apparently equated with identification with a political party? Are the labors of a Treasury senior civil servant to elaborate and make effective a tax policy of a President to be deemed equivalent to campaigning for the Democratic or Republican Party? More than a few officials and commentators have been baffled by the "strange image of a projected senior civil service" living in an "uncertain and emotionless limbo," [1] as well as the "appalling confusion between party politics and policy politics." [2]

The Commission and Task Force could not have intended the oddities evoked by a literal interpretation of their text. What then were they driving at?

5

PRESIDENT'S MEN AND CAREER OFFICERS

They reaffirmed the necessity of a career merit system in the sense projected by the civil service reformers of the 1880's and renewed by the President's Committee on

[1] Stephen Bailey: "The President and His Political Executives," 307 *Annals Amer. Acad. Pol. and Soc. Sci.* (Sept., 1956), p. 33.
[2] Harlan Cleveland: "The Executive and the Public Interest," 307 *Annals Amer. Acad. Pol. and Soc. Sci.* (Sept., 1956), p. 52.

THE THINGS THAT ARE CAESAR'S

Administrative Management of 1937. They focused upon
the higher levels of the civil administration whose distinctive significance had eluded the early reformers. They
rejected the aspiration of nineteenth-century reformers,
endorsed by the President's Committee of 1937, toward
an absorption of almost the entire Executive Branch into
the civil service excepting only the "highest [posts] such
as the members of the Cabinet and the ministers to
foreign countries." [3] They rejected it on principle, not as
a sop to assumed pressures of practical politics. They
believed a career civil service insufficient as an exclusive
instrument of administration, however indispensable its
contribution as a part.

Consciously or not, the second Hoover Commission
ranged itself in accord with strictures voiced concerning
the career services of Britain by Walter Bagehot and
Stafford Northcote in the nineteenth century and Harold
Nicolson, Lord Chief Justice Hewart, and occasional
Labor critics in the twentieth. In Chapter V, I referred to
their criticisms. With varying emphasis, they deplored
tendencies to which they considered a hierarchical career
service in Britain to be prone. Bagehot feared it would
incline to stodginess, unadaptability and preoccupation
with trivia. Northcote and Hewart suspected that it
would suck power from the proper custodians of political
power, "working like gravity by night and by day, gaining
a little today and a little tomorrow. . . ." [4] Nicolson was

[3] Annual Report of the U.S. Civil Service Commission
(1890–91), p. 15.
[4] From a letter of Thomas Jefferson, who was expressing his
fears of a comparable tendency which he believed he could

212

concerned about a penchant to overemphasize criteria and methods made irrelevant by time and change. Some Labor politicians and commentators were apprehensive lest career officers serve poorly the policies of a sector of the populace newly risen to power, because of an identification of the higher levels of the services with a particular social class.

The class factor has played no part in American attitudes towards the Civil Service; and if the Foreign Service at times has not been entirely free of popular or Congressional suspicion in this regard, it has been a minor and diminishing irritant. But bureaucratic inertia involves a special risk in the United States, superimposed upon the universal aspects of the hazard. The special element derives from the constitutional separation of the President and Congress and the nature of American political parties.

A working association between a bureau chief of long tenure and a chairman of a congressional committee whose recurrent re-election tends to be assured by the predominance of one party in his district or state can erect litle Gilbraltars of resistance to change. To a new President seeking to institute new measures, the resistance can be formidable, however great his majority or clear his popular mandate. The national government can be energetic only if the President plays his indispensable role as a sort of prime mover. The strength of a British

discern in the federal judiciary. Jefferson to Charles Hammond, Aug. 18, 1821, in *The Writings of Thomas Jefferson*, ed. Lipscomb and Bergh (Thomas Jefferson Memorial Assn., 1905), XV–XVI, pp. 330, 331–2.

Prime Minister's leadership of his party in Parliament is rooted not only in the nature of parliamentary government but more especially in his control of the machinery of a unitary political party. A Prime Minister of Britain can seldom be matched in this regard by an American President, whatever the latter's political force and skill. A President also stands at the head of his party. But his party is a federation of the parties of fifty states, loosely organized except once in four years during a presidential election. A general awareness of the conditions has bred a school of thought, today preponderant among American politicians and students of administration, that holds the capacity of a President to do his job dependent upon his freedom to appoint "President's men" in sufficient number to key posts. The second Hoover Commission and the Task Force in effect aligned themselves with this view, making room for the "President's men" in the category of political executives.

One may feel an itch of doubt concerning the Commission's and Task Force's rationale. Apart from the sober and scholarly accent, how does the doctrine of the political executive differ in spirit from the brusque pronouncement of Binger Hermann, Commissioner of the Land Office in 1898, that the Civil Service must be excluded from the confidential and political functions of the administration and confined to the "justly clerical"? [5] A matter-of-fact politician-administrator, Hermann acknowledged the advent of the Civil Service and the political weight of the reformers. He was prepared to

[5] See Chapter VII, p. 160, n. 3.

allot a sphere to them, provided it did not impinge unduly upon the more important or at least the juicier jobs. When Senator Hoar of Massachusetts on the Senate floor in 1889 proposed to apply the then new Civil Service Act to "every official . . . whose duties were not of a political or a confidential nature and whom it was not expedient to have in sympathy with the administration when that administration was carrying out its political theories and policies in regard to which its opponents would be expected not to be in sympathy," [6] was he talking the language of Binger Hermann or the Task Force on Personnel and Civil Service of the second Hoover Commission?

In the United States today, even the most hard-bitten of the men who win political power on the national scene (however large a residue of Neanderthalism may persist in local government) understand that they must pass beyond a bare acquisition and exercise of political power to the conduct of government. Feeling the scale and complexity of the job, aware that its requirements have long since ceased to be "plain and simple," sensing that margins for error have narrowed, they accept the need to use men qualified to govern, at best with conviction, at least as a fact of political life. What more natural than their preference to make their own choice of men so qualified? A President and his closest party-political aides will want a free hand to make their own appointments up to a certain point, even if the sheer magnitude of the national government's roster of civil employees, number-

[6] 20 Cong. Rec., Part 2 (Fiftieth Cong., 2d Sess.), p. 1608.

ing 2,491,791 in 1964, can exhaust their appetite and dispose them to welcome assistance from career personnel services in large areas. Does the concept of the political executive boil down to an attempt to put a doctrinal face upon an acceptance of this fact?

To an extent, I believe it does; and to the extent that it does, I believe it neither weak nor specious, but wise and honest. For a workable accommodation between the exigencies of political power and the conduct of government, an institutional setting is necessary that recognizes the position of the men who can win and hold political power as well as the operating requirements of the men who can govern. The concept of the political executive, given effect in established practice and limited by the parallel insistence upon the role of senior civil servants, can contribute to such an institutional setting. It has an added value, in emphasizing that a system of appointments based on character and talent is practicable apart from a career merit system of the technical sort. There is a risk that Presidents may be pushed by the job-hungry toward an increment of party-political appointments among the policy-political, but in the conditions of government at the national level in the United States today, the risk can be contained. Even if the second Hoover Commission pressed the complementary concepts of political executive and senior civil servant beyond the point where they could be useful and obscured the core with dubious refinements, we would be foolish to forfeit the substance.

The absolute separation of political executives and

senior career officers envisaged by the second Hoover Commission has not been supported by other comparable bodies charged with comparable responsibilities. The Committee on Foreign Affairs Personnel of 1961–62 (the Herter Committee), surveying "personnel for the new diplomacy," contemplated an open competition among career foreign service officers and citizen candidates for "top executive posts" in the conduct of foreign affairs. Emphasizing that political leadership in foreign affairs "must be undergirded by professional career services," the Committee continued:

The use of career public servants in filling top executive posts raises an important issue of public policy which the Committee believes merits special comment. The Committee takes it as self-evident that the President must and will have freedom to choose from the entire national pool of qualified men and women in selecting key appointive officials in foreign affairs. Career officers should constitute a prime resource within the national pool. They should receive no less consideration than others as potential choices for the highest executive posts; they should neither enjoy an automatic priority nor suffer from an adverse presumption. Rather they should be deemed available and encouraged to aspire to such posts with the knowledge that they will be appraised in competition with others drawn from any part of the nation's human resources. They can ask or expect no more. If the quality, training, and experience of career officers

217

are steadily upgraded as recommended in this report, increasing numbers of them are bound to be selected for high executive posts at home as well as abroad.

This concept is consistent with, and does no violence to, the principle of Presidential control. Political direction must, of course, emanate from the President, but political direction need not conflict with the need for depth of experience in, and professional knowledge of, foreign affairs, whether acquired within or outside the career services. Whoever is appointed to positions of top executive responsibility must enjoy the confidence of the responsible political head—the President, the Secretary of State, or heads of other foreign affairs agencies, as the case may be. Those so appointed must also be prepared to accept the political hazards implicit in these positions.[7]

Since Lyndon Johnson acceded to the presidency on November 23, 1963, he has turned increasingly to John Macy, Chairman of the Civil Service Commission, for assistance in appointments throughout the civil administration. In advising the President in the search for talent, Mr. Macy has served in a role separate from his duties as Chairman of the Civil Service Commission. In his own terms and along his own distinctive lines, the President has hewn to a course in appointments for the entire national administration similar to that independently advocated by the Committee on Foreign Affairs Personnel

[7] Report of the Committee on Foreign Affairs Personnel (published under the auspices of the Carnegie Endowment for International Peace, Washington, D.C., Dec., 1962), pp. 7–8.

for the administration of foreign affairs. At a press conference on March 20, 1965, President Johnson stated:

> Since November, 1963, I have made a total of 163 major appointments through today. Of the 135 nonjudicial appointments, almost exactly half—49 per cent —have been purely merit appointments made from the career services of the Government or other Government background. Fourteen per cent, additionally, have come from university careers, 16 per cent from business and labor, 19 per cent from the legal profession and, I would like to add, they have included both Republicans and Democrats.[8]

As a point more intriguing than important, we may note in passing that the several percentage figures cited by the President came to a sum of 98 per cent. The unexplained remainder may represent a patronage component or possibly a flaw in the arithmetic of the presidential staff.

While Chairman Macy has striven to strengthen the career services in domestic administration as the Herter Committee sought to do in foreign affairs, neither has seen any need for so opaque a demarcation between career appointments and other appointments based on merit as was advocated by the second Hoover Commission. Nor has President Johnson. Explicitly avowing that a consistent record of accomplishment in the Executive

[8] *The New York Times,* March 21, 1965, p. 70.

Branch depends upon "the ability and the integrity . . . of the men and women who serve" it, and being "determined that the American people shall be served by the very best talent available," [9] President Johnson appears to have sought the "best talent" through a mix of career personnel and political executives. The nature of the mix has not yet fully emerged.

6

A POTENTIAL ACCOMMODATION

In current doctrine and practice at the national level, there are potentialities for an accommodation that would fit the special American and contemporary features as well as the universal and timeless aspects of the interaction between men who can win political power and men who can govern. The accommodation could be realized by giving effect to the concept of political executives in an established pattern of appointments, broadening the concept of a career service, applying imagination and energy in recruitment for both categories, and adjusting the mix.

Political executives should be chosen by the President on the basis of general and special criteria. The general criteria would be integrity and ability. The special criterion would be identification with the President's purposes and policies. The President should convass all sources in recruitment, outside and inside the government. Eye-

[9] Ibid.

brows need not be raised if among those qualified according to the criteria, a President should tend to prefer men belonging to his own political party. The political executives would not only serve the needs contemplated by the second Hoover Commission but would help to satisfy the imperatives of public administration in America revealed through Andrew Jackson: a popular sense of identification with the civil administration and the fact of popular participation in it. I do not imply that career services are inherently inconsistent with the Jacksonian imperatives. On the contrary, when a career service is open to all on the same conditions of merit, and when the fulfillment of potentialities for merit is fostered by universal opportunities for education, a people can regard the career service as its own. But the populace can identify themselves more vividly with President's men, drawn more immediately from the society and more recently in touch with trends of opinion and change. The appointment of political executives involves an interchange that brings talented citizens into government and experienced public officers back into private citizenship. The reciprocal flow in the appointive sector represents a distinctive American contribution to the art of democratic government. It enriches the government with diversified experience and fresh angles of vision, and it informs public opinion through the presence among the citizenry of fellow citizens familiar with the government from the inside.

Though these are attributes to be treasured, they are not enough. There are limits to what an amateur can do, however gifted he may be. There are limits to what a transient in government can do, even when he is professional in training and experience. The limits are even sharper when the incumbent is both a transient and an amateur. There are also limits to the turnover in personnel that can be borne by an organization.

A complementary element is needed of men selected by the same general but different special criteria. The general criteria again would be character and talent. The special criteria would be continuity, commitment, and special skill, the essence of a career service. I speak of "continuity, commitment, and special skill" rather than "career service" to stress the essentials and avoid implications of any particular form. I have referred to a tendency in American usage to equate "career service" with one kind of career corps, involving regular recruitment at a uniform entering level and advancement through grades, as in the Civil Service or the Foreign Service. Such a career system, admirable for many purposes, represents only one pattern through which continuity, commitment, and expertise may be assured in government service.

The federal judiciary in the United States and the judiciary of Britain exemplify another pattern, and the faculties of American state universities still another. A Justice of the Supreme Court of the United States may be appointed from the next level in the federal judicial hierarchy or as readily from a state court, a faculty of law, or the practicing bar. The faculty of a state university may be recruited at the lowest grade as teaching assistants or instructors, to be promoted through regular steps in a ladder of ranks, but they may also be enrolled directly as assistant professors, associate professors, or professors. Professors may be chosen as freely from the faculties of other state or private universities or, less typically, from the professions, government, or industry, as from the lower ranks within the same state university. Standards of merit in selection are observed no less rigorously, relevant expertise is no less distinguished, commitment to the job no less profound, and continuity no less marked in the federal judiciary or the faculties of state universities than in other government career lines.

The United States Civil Service and the Foreign Service are indispensable. They must be supported in terms of their own structures and functions, and it will be wise to extend them from time to time in selected areas. But it need not be assumed that the essence of career service can only be realized through the extension of the Civil Service and the Foreign Service upward, outward, and downward to embrace all sectors of the civil administration other than those reserved for political executives. The substance of continuity—a problem treated by a man who handled it in earlier phases and will be on hand if the problem recurs, the substance of commitment— devotion to a job by a man who sees it as his primary interest and life's work, and the substance of expertise— relevant skill acquired through study or experience, must be distinguished from this or that form in which they may be incorporated. The career element in the civil administration may be represented by variant systems. New variants may prove especially appropriate for certain types of scientific, technical and professional personnel needed by the government.

What of the proportions between the political executive and career elements, measured by the members in each category who meet the general criteria of quality as well as the special criteria of the category? At the higher levels of the civil administration, I suggest we do not have the right mix. The political executives make up too large a part of the aggregate. In the higher executive and professional posts, the career component in the broad sense should be enlarged.

It is impossible to offer figures for the right mix. The government of the United States is too complex an organic growth and the teeming currents of American life too full of phenomena to be compressible within measurements or formulas. Opportunities must be sought steadily to increase the proportion of men whose ability and character are reinforced by continuity, commitment and expertise. It is a matter of emphasis and direction, animated by a conviction of need, and sustained long enough for the emphasis to take root in American folkways.

I believe that an accommodation between the realities of political power and the needs of government can be achieved along the lines here projected, at the national level. While neither imminent nor easy, it does not lie beyond the reach of the present generation of Americans.

224

7

UNFINISHED BUSINESS AND BEYOND

Even if and when the accommodation here envisaged should be achieved, an arduous prospect would remain in local government. The potential accommodation in the national government may be identified as critical unfinished business for America. At the local level, the need for a corresponding accommodation is acute, but it would stretch optimism to the breaking point to regard the business of accommodation as merely unfinished. It is business scarcely begun.

Since the turn of the century and Theodore Roosevelt's "Square Deal" and "New Nationalism," it has been the central internal task of government in the United States to realize the opportunities and contain the stresses of modern technology and economic organization while vindicating the heritage of freedom. The opportunities and the strains reach a peak in our cities.

. . . the more crowded people have become in cities the more they have craved both security and freedom. . . .

Thus urban crowding and the slums and mobs characteristic of it may be considered growing pains in the endless process of civilization.

In the same way, the picture of Megalopolis [the almost continuous stretch of urban and suburban areas from southern New Hampshire to northern

225

Virginia and from the Atlantic shore to the Appalachian foothills] is not as dark as the outspoken pessimists and frequent protests would seem to paint it. Crowded within its limits is an extremely distinguished population. It is, on the *average,* the richest, best educated, best housed, and best serviced group of similar size . . . in the world. . . . It is true that many of its sections have seen pretty rural landscapes replaced by ugly industrial agglomerations or drab and monstrous residential developments; it is true that in many parts of Megalopolis the air is not clean any more, the noise is disturbing day and night, the water is not as pure as one would wish, and transportation at times becomes a nightmare. . . .

. . . Megalopolis stands indeed at the threshold of a new way of life, and upon solution of its problems will rest civilization's ability to survive. . . . [Material in brackets added.] [1]

Needs and defects in primary and secondary education, racial tensions, traffic congestion, water shortages, decay in housing, slums, crime and delinquency, coming to a head in the cities, fall primarily or largely within the province of local governments, at least in the first instance. And thereby hangs an ironic tale. Government in the cities and towns of America has its heroes and heroines, typically unsung, too often serving in thankless conditions. It involves no disregard of our debt to them to recognize that the cities and towns typically represent the

[1] J. Gottmann: *Megalopolis* (New York: The Twentieth Century Fund; 1961), 14–16.

most weakly manned sector of government in the United States. Yet the jobs which local governments are expected to do, alone or with aid or supervision from the national or state governments, could be decisive in settling the temper of American life. At times and in places, the discrepancy in local government between the kind of men needed to do a job and the kind who get the job can stagger the most sanguine observer.

The lines of accommodation projected in this book from the American experience of national government might also prove applicable in local government. Or they might not, however fully they should be vindicated at the national level. In no event could their transferability to the local sector be taken for granted. The lessons distilled from the national experience can serve as a background for understanding. Against that background, the seeds for an accommodation in local government must be sought chiefly in the structure, processes, and history of American urban society itself. We may take Walt Whitman's injunction to heart: "Now understand me well—it is provided in the essence of things, that from any fruition of success, no matter what, shall come forth something to make a greater struggle necessary." [2]

[2] "Song of the Open Road," 16, in *Leaves of Grass* (New York: Grosset & Dunlap), p. 197.

INDEX

Adams, Brooks, 178

Adams, John: Maclay, 169–70; appointments, 172, 174; "gentlemen," 172–5; checks and balances, 173–4; concept of democracy, 173–4, 179

Adams, John Quincy, 178

administration, interaction with policy, 153, 156, 209–11

Adoula, Cyrille, 56

Africa: new states, 43; self-assertion, 44

A.I.D., 207

Agricultural Stabilization and Conservation Service, 206

American political parties, 168, 171–2, 217–18, ch. vii–viii *passim*

American Revolution: interaction with French and Industrial revolutions, 29, 30, 45, 82–3; effect in developing states, 45; effect in Germany, 129, 131, 133

Anne (Queen of Eng.), 76

Antoninus Pius, 21

Area Redevelopment Administration, 206

Aristotle, 11

Arthur, Chester A., 147–8

Asst. Sec'y of State for International Organization Affairs, 207

Asst. Sec'y of State for Public Affairs, 207

Atomic Energy Commission, 207

Bagehot, Walter, 88, 102, 216

Barker, Ernest, 114, 128

Belgium: military forces in Congo, 48; Katanga, 48–9; Congo independence, 48, 60

Ben Bella, Ahmed, 58

Berkeley, Judge, 112–13

Bernadotte, Marshal, 38

Bismarck: and William I, 108; view of parliament, 109; use of civil service, 110, 133; comparison with Laud, 111; social legislation, 133–4

Bonaparte, Charles J., 149

Bonaparte, Lucien, 36

i

A NOTE ABOUT THE AUTHOR

Milton Katz writes from a background of diversified experience in government, foreign affairs, education, law and civic affairs. Since 1954 he has been Henry L. Stimson Professor of Law and Director of International Legal Studies at Harvard. In 1950–1, he served as chief of the Marshall Plan in Europe, with the rank of ambassador, and as the U. S. Representative on the Economic Commission for Europe. From 1951 to 1953 he was Associate Director of the Ford Foundation. Earlier in his career he served as Byrne Professor of Administrative Law at Harvard; with the Securities and Exchange Commission, the Department of Justice, the War Production Board, and the Office of Strategic Services; and as a Lt. Commander, USNR, in World War II. He is a trustee of the Carnegie Endowment for International Peace, Brandeis University, the Citizens' Research Foundation; and a Fellow of the American Academy of Arts and Sciences. In 1961–2 he was a member of the Herter Committee on Foreign Affairs Personnel.

A NOTE ON THE TYPE

The Text of this book was set on the Linotype in a new face called PRIMER, designed by RUDOLPH RUZICKA, earlier responsible for the design of Fairfield and Fairfield Medium, Linotype faces whose virtues have for some time now been accorded wide recognition.

The complete range of sizes of Primer was first made available in 1954, although the pilot size of 12 point was ready as early as 1951. The design of the face makes general reference to Linotype Century (long a serviceable type, totally lacking in manner or frills of any kind) but brilliantly corrects the characterless quality of that face.

Typography and binding design by

GEORGE SALTER